Intentional Mastery

Intentional Mastery

Step beyond your expertise and

Build Better Business

William Buist

Intentional Mastery

ISBN 978-1-912300-62-4

eISBN 978-1-912300-63-1

Published in 2022 by SRA Books

Printed in the UK

A CIP record of this book is available from the British Library.

Contents

Foreword   vii

Introduction   1

Section 1: The Beginnings of Mastery

1 Building Better Business   13

2 Mastery   23

3 Better on Purpose   45

Section 2: Masterful Strategies

4 Some Thoughts on Strategy   67

5 Self   77

6 Skills   111

7 Systems   127

8 Sales   139

9 Signposting   149

Section 3: Mastering Joy

10 Making a Difference   163

11 Taking Intentional Decisions and Actions   175

12 Sharing Insights and Skills   187

13 Being Yourself   201

14 What's Next?   209

Afterword – Making a Dent   215

Acknowledgements   219

Foreword

William Buist first crossed my path in 2015, when I joined a small group of entrepreneurs and business owners to share insights on how to tackle business problems and make the most of opportunities. When you're busy it can be difficult to take time out to work on your business rather than being immersed in it. I'll be honest. As I strolled along Pall Mall, I was wondering whether I really had time for this. What a great decision I made to invest the time that day! William facilitated the session superbly and shared insights that were thought provoking and based upon solid experience in the world of business. I implemented my first idea from working with this group straight away.

This was to be the first of many meetings involving William over the years. I can always rely on him to share an insight that transforms an issue I'm dealing with. To this day I am still working with William when the need arises. He is now helping to develop my leadership team to rise to the challenges of a business that is growing again, following the worldwide pandemic.

Reading this book is like having access to William's mentoring skills at your fingertips. Whether you already run a successful business or you are just starting out, this book will help you discover what shapes your thinking, change your mindset and move you forward to make your unique difference in the world.

It starts by exploring how to 'build better business' and how this links to mastery, purpose and legacy. 'Better' is a term used a lot in my business in relation to improving what we do. For me, as a leader this means creating a culture where people can challenge with support and respect.

Every new challenge that a business faces brings with it an opportunity to improve. Only with an open environment where people can say 'This needs to be better' can you find a way to deliver something that truly works in helping people build skills and confidence at work.

Reading William's book has inspired me to think of more ways to encourage mastery in every person within the business. When you relate the concepts to your life and work you will find many ideas that will inspire you to discover mastery and, ultimately, leave behind your own legacy.

William introduces us to the concept of 'mastering joy'. This is very close to my heart. Running a business for me has always had at the core the idea of helping people to develop skills and grow in confidence. Reading this book may also provide the spark you need to discover and bring to life what motivates you to master joy and make a meaningful difference.

This book captures many of the insights I have gained from every interaction I have had with William. I've seen how he has worked with other clients, helping them to solve their business problems, understand themselves in a deeper way and build better business. The book is packed full of ideas that will help you to become a master of your business too.

Amanda Vickers

CEO, Speak First

www.speak-first.com

Introduction

A lifetime before I started writing this book, I took my first job. I started in August 1980, right in the middle of a deep recession. Inflation was running at 18 per cent or so, and unemployment was rising fast. It was clear in 1980 that the rise was set to continue for some time, and by 1983 it had peaked at 11.3 per cent of the working population. Interest rates were just below their eye-watering peak of 17 per cent at the end of 1979. It was a very different environment from the one we find ourselves in today, yet there were many parallels.

My boss – and later, my mentor – Bill, was a master in his field. He had the courage to hire me in that environment and, when he did (on an initial salary of £3,600), my father breathed a sigh of relief. His boy had got a career, or at least he thought he had. I knew then, as I know now, that the world that rises out of the ashes of economic shocks is always very different from the one that went before. My father's experience was of being sent to work in Blackley, Manchester for the then chemicals giant Imperial Chemical Industries (ICI) by the war office in the middle of the Second World War. He worked in a world where those who worked hard and gave their loyalty to an employer were rewarded with promotion. If they wanted it, employers would employ their best staff for life and build a suitable pension to ensure that they and their families were safe and secure in retirement. But by 1980 the world was changing. The economy was shifting from manufacturing to services. It's why I could find employment in insurance, while markets like the motor industry, the steel industry and mining were declining rapidly.

I started to ask questions to try to understand why that happened: why some markets thrived and others withered, what made some get better and others worse. I started asking questions and, over the years since, many have been answered.

Bill wisely observed that, in recessions, most companies become cautious about investment. They trim back spending and look more carefully at protecting their profitability. 'But,' he observed, 'some only restrict the number of projects and other activities that they work on rather than restricting the spending on everything. Spending on the projects those companies choose to maintain often goes up, not down. They look for quality – not speed – and decision making may take longer, yet it is more robust.'

Ten years later I'd changed companies, the United Kingdom had changed government, and another recession gripped the country. This time I saw for myself what Bill had told me. I saw that those companies that focused on quality, that had clarity of purpose – that could describe what they did and could prove how well they did it – were growing in the recessions. They were raising prices, building better business and making more reliable profits. So many of the others used pricing as a lever, slashing prices to try to attract business, cutting corners, yet still losing out.

'Better' is one of those words that has different meanings to different people at different times. It depends on context and your current situation. Throughout this book I will talk about 'building better business', and I think it is important to consider each of these words briefly so that I align your understanding with my intention.

I've been running a small business for a long time, and if there is one enduring thing I've learned, it is that no two days are the same – at least not exactly. It seems we are always working to make changes because we continue to gather experience and knowledge that we didn't have before – at least if we have pride in our work. That new experience, the additional knowledge, the honed skills are like bricks, and as we add them we are building anew. 'Building' refers to that continual change.

'Better' means that today's business is different today from how it was in the past. That difference is better if it meets your terms for improvement. There isn't a definition of better that works in all circumstances. Your 'better' is not my 'better' – yet you probably know instinctively what your better is.

Finally, I've used 'business' in a loose sense. Anything from a hobby that occasionally pays you (like my love of photography) to your magnum opus – the most important work of your lifetime – can benefit from the principles and ideas contained in this book.

For me, 'better business' has an honesty about it. When someone is striving to be better, they have to be vulnerable too; they have to be willing to hush their ego and listen with humility to what they need to change. They also need to understand what the business needs in order to change. That is the alignment I spoke of earlier. 'Building better' means creating something different and yet familiar, built on foundations that are solid, that has strong values and that communicates them well.

Realising that being vulnerable (and showing that honestly) demonstrates both power and humility was pivotal. I realised that to recognise that there was a better business to be built meant accepting what I had was not as good as it could be. It meant that, in time, I would look back and see it as worse. I had to accept that I had to change. Notice, I am not saying 'I had to change the business'; I am saying 'I had to change' and yet, in the moment I did not know what to do or how. That was both frightening and magical. The hairs on the back of my neck stood up, my curiosity was piqued and I began to focus on building better business. I have never looked back.

In the years since then I've seen boom times and tough times. I've made mistakes – some howlers – errors of omission and errors of commission too. Yet I have also had some great successes, of which I am proud. Through it all I've seen that there are common actions that great businesses do well all the time, and the best – the wiser ones, perhaps – stick to in the tough times. As my understanding of the implications of building better business grew, I started to see that those business owners who were most at ease with the businesses they led had a common trait: they had something more than expertise; they had something quite special. They had a presence in their markets, humble confidence from a deep knowledge of their topic, honed skills and deep experience, and they were insightful beyond measure. Masters of their subjects.

Some of these are obvious, but how to achieve them is more subtle. The important elements are here in this book, so that you can see what it will take for you to be the master of your art, and so that you can enjoy that journey for all it will bring you. If you choose to start to become a master of what you do as a result of reading this book, you will also be building better business every day.

What is mastery?

One of the lessons that Bill taught me was that there are elements of mastery all around us, and in each of us – if only we can harness it, work at it, understand it and develop it. When you do, there's something special that happens not just for you, the master, but for all of those you touch.

David Adrian Smith is one such master, and his journey provides a rich tapestry of what's involved and why it matters. Let's explore that story together.

With a common name, David Smith wisely chose to invoke his middle name so as to ensure that there was no confusion when people spoke of him. His career began in 1984, aged 16, when he left school. He was apprenticed for five years with Gordon Farr, a traditional sign-writer, who had mastered the skill of painting letters. As David learned from him, he too became a letter painter and a pictorialist. In 1992, David set up his own business in Torquay, and his unique design and pristine execution style became his, and his alone. But it was not yet what it is today.

During a visit to New Zealand, he was invited to California to meet Rick Glawson of the famous Fine Gold Sign Company. Rick was known as the godfather of gilding. He had a passion to share his encyclopaedic knowledge of glass decoration with others who were studying the craft.

The two men became firm friends. David made a commitment to attend the California Conclave of Letterheads every year.[1] This is a meeting of talented sign artists, carvers, muralists and gold leaf experts. David's passion for creating elaborate,

1 'California Conclave 2000 – Hand Lettering Forum'. Available at: www. handletteringforum.com/forum/viewtopic.php?t=3976 accessed 14/06/2021.

ornate mirrors and reverse glass signs of distinction was fuelled by seeing the expertise and skill on show at these meetings. Ultimately, sign-writing wasn't where David's real passion lay, and so he sold his business to concentrate more fully on gilding, painting and acid-etching glass. He learned the skills needed to add brilliant cutting in order to reach the mastery of replicating the Victorian glass work he so admired. Still based in Devon, David is now running workshops, training courses and remote one-to-one support on the phone to pass on those skills to others, protecting them for the future. In that way, he can repay the debt he feels he owes to Gordon Farr, Rick Glawson and others too numerous to mention, for their generosity in sharing their knowledge and passion with him.

There is much here that signposts the journey to mastery that we can all take – though few will. David did not set out to be a master. Rather, he explored his capabilities and honed them. In doing so he found elements he was good at and enjoyed. It was through the encouragement and ideas of those who supported him that David saw what was possible with the skills he was honing. It was through his growing expertise that David realised that he now needed to step up again. To pass on those skills, he needed to gain the insights to understand and pass on his talent and, importantly, his unique interpretation of it. That is mastery.

I hope in this book to give you insights into what it will take to become the master you can be. David recognised that his sign-writing skills were too generic, and that led him to sell the successful business he was running in order to master a niche within it. It is also a warning to those of us who think we can serve anyone, or who feel uneasy narrowing our skills to a single detail. But to be a master, we must. We will return to this in Chapter 2.

Building better business through mastery

It isn't every day that the hairs on the back of your neck stand up and your throat goes dry because of a single thought. A thought that clears the fog, that uncovers insights you'd been seeking for years.

I remember one such day for me as clearly as if it was yesterday. I was blown away by the impact it had. I was out walking on a warm and sunny spring day, musing about a business issue a client was having around their strategic intentions. As I contemplated their situation, I realised that there were many parallels with my own (aren't there always?). Suddenly what had been opaque for them (and for me) fell into place. They were already good at what they did and had a great reputation, but to maintain the business required hard work – lots of it – and it was constraining them and their ability to truly build the business they wanted. I'd been thinking about some, just a few, of the businesspeople I know who are truly masterful at what they do. It was during that walk, step by step, that I began to see what those masters had achieved and, importantly, how we can all do so too, if we choose to. I knew where my client's future path to building better business through mastery lay.

And then… I also learned something quite profound about my own business – so much of what I had been working toward had aligned. I had a clarity and insight that had only arrived now because I had finally mastered a particular way of working. Much that I knew about my business had seemed somehow separate and disconnected. Now it joined up. Why? Because I could see how it all supported one single, vital common purpose. Has that happened for you?

One consequence of having a single common purpose is the realisation that the business and one's own life are synergistically more successful when both are aligned. They are both most successful when they have the same focus. The whole is truly much greater than the sum of the parts. This book is about how to achieve that synchronicity, that mastery.

It's no surprise, looking back, that I can identify that day, that moment. It was the one day my life changed. While much was immediately clearer, what was exciting to me was that I knew that much more could become clearer later. I was eager with anticipation and excited by the opportunities. I'd recognised what mastery really was, and in that moment, on that morning, the seeds for the writing of this book were planted.

Nothing is unconnected, yet the connections can be subtle – an almost invisible, gossamer thread that binds one thing to the next. I think one role we can all have in life is to understand the strands that matter (to us), wherever they flow: in business; in ourselves; with those we love, and beyond – and then to strive to make them ever stronger.

About you

In the foregoing you've seen through my own story and that of David Adrian Smith how the fortunes of business and your own understanding, skill, experience and insight – your own mastery – are intimately linked.

You might read this book because you know that you want to start building better business. Your business won't be broken, yet you know that it could be so much better. You're looking for the clues that might lead you to make business changes that will lift the performance of the business, that will make it better. You will find ways to do that in these pages. Section 1 provides an introduction to mastery, and provides the context for building better business and doing so intentionally. Section 2 focuses on your business, and when you follow the strategies you will create a more certain, more predictable, reliable business as a result. Section 3 brings together the impact of mastery for you and bringing joy to your work, before concluding by discussing 'what's next'.

You might also read this book because you know that you want to attain your own mastery. Maybe you've developed great skills and are already known as an expert in your field, yet that field is crowded with others who do what you do, and also have expertise. You want to stand out as the master of what you do.

You, your business, your mastery, building better business – all are intertwined. As a business leader it's not possible to separate them. In the stories that follow you will see, as you have already seen from the journey of David Adrian Smith, that mastery is at the pinnacle of business strategy and personal insight.

Section 1

The Beginnings of Mastery

Every meaningful decision has context: the context of the information used to inform the decision, and the context of the consequences of making that decision. Deciding that you wish to develop your own mastery is a life-changing decision (and, for all those who make it, a life-affirming one). I wouldn't be doing justice to you, the reader, if we didn't clarify that context first.

We'll explore some foundations in this section:

1. First we'll discuss how to build better business, in Chapter 1 (page 13).

2. Then we will dig into what mastery really is in Chapter 2 (page 23).

3. Then we will look at foundations in Chapter 3 (page 45).

1 **Building Better Business**

I only feel angry when I see waste.

– Mother Theresa

The start

This book came about because of waste. The waste of time, effort and energy of thousands of business owners – people whose determination and commitment to using their skills brought them to the decision to run their own businesses and to make a difference for others. We are a relatively unusual group of people – perhaps 5 per cent of the population, or less. We are keen, in the main, to use our knowledge, skills and experience with professionalism and pride. We strive to bring new value for others to the forefront, to be paid a fair return for our effort and to be building better business every day. When this is done well, everybody wins: you, your clients, society as a whole. Yet for many and much of the time, that effort, determination and focus can simply fail to achieve what you expected, and your time, energy and money go to waste.

Let's look at what happens.

Running a business isn't just about doing the thing we are good at; we need a solid business to deliver the work, and we have to communicate what we do to others. We seek to attract those for whom what we do will add value. We ask them first to consider our offer and then we ask them to decide to buy it. We have to be able to deliver our service and manage all the administration. Waste can creep in all too easily in the form of missed opportunities, inefficiency, stress and fear that debilitates and enervates. Too often I've seen businesspeople work long (really long) hours. They may be struggling to make ends meet, week after week, month after month, or they may not; yet, they've found efficiencies that others in their market rely on. For some, the business swallows every waking hour, leaving no time for hobbies, relaxation or the family. For others there's a constant level of stress that eats away at the business owner, leaving them a diminished shadow of what they could be. That's the waste that drives me to write this book. It's not an inevitable part of running a business, however much it seems so. Let's end it!

Some business owners chose a path that deliberately shifted them from being employees to running a business. For others the choice was not theirs – at least initially – perhaps through redundancy or the closure of their employer's business. For a few it is the only path they've ever known.

For those of us who do run our own businesses, it takes courage to live with the level of uncertainty about what the future may hold. Yet, however you came to be a business owner, from that day to this you will have been striving to do good work, to meet the needs of your customers, and to feed your family and save for the future. Striving, but perhaps not always succeeding.

I've worked with business owners for much of my working life and have run my own business supporting and advising business owners since 2004. In that time I've been struck by two things. First, in many (but not all) businesses, a desire to do *better* business and second, an intention to be a master of the art of what you do.

Those two things alone are not enough. Business isn't just about what you do. As every business owner knows, they also need to be able to deliver the other aspects of running a business: marketing, sales, operations, finance and so on. Very few business owners are good at everything, and no one who has also reached mastery in their chosen specialism is. No one. So, the good news is that you don't have to be competent in every aspect of running your business, and trying to be will always constrain you. This is where the waste emerges, and why this book is here.

When people are asked why they do what they do, listen carefully – the answers will often address a desire to improve and to be uniquely positioned in a market. Building better business and mastery together. While we may be passionate about achieving both outcomes, is it because of taking the same action in the hope of creating both that we, too often, come up short? One aspect of mastery is knowing that building better business and mastery itself are different yet synergistic ambitions. The desire and the intention to set off on the journey to achieve both are necessary for your business to thrive. I must warn you, though – desire and intention on their own are not sufficient.

Successful businesses have clear strategies in five areas: around the business owner (self), delivering with panache (skills), being efficient and effective (systems), finding customers (sales) and communications (signposting). These strategies provide the foundation of building better business.

Great strategy alone isn't enough. This book will allow you to understand what you are currently doing, show you the gaps and describe a strategic approach to fill them. Bringing them all together will allow you to be building better business every day. In implementing the strategies you will also gain experience and uncover the insights that will help you understand where you need to take action to develop mastery of what you do.

Let's start.

How we got here

First, let's just reflect for a moment on the journey to where we are, as that will help us to understand the trajectory, to see where we are heading and the decisions we need to make in a wide context.

The world has seen so much change as humanity has found ways to harness the resources at its disposal and to collaborate (something we'll discuss further in Chapter 6) in order to push the boundaries of what is possible. Humankind has struggled simply to survive in a difficult world. For a long time, hunting and gathering food was the extent of life. Yet we learned to farm, and that meant we could settle in one place. Then we learned to build and harness the power of the natural world. In doing so we sought to learn and improve, and gradually we industrialised. Today, now our technology has miniaturised, we focus more on data and electrons and less on muscle and ploughshares.

Yet in all those ages - every one - what's been rewarded has been specialisms. Being extremely good at one thing. Whether that was predicting the weather, understanding where the animals you hunted would be, building steam engines, harnessing the wind, or analysing data; being the master of your art, your particular skill, was the pinnacle of success. Those who got to that pinnacle have always been revered, protected and supported. They survived and passed on the genes that make specialism a great survival tactic.

For hunter-gatherers, that was served best by loyalty to the tribe. In the agricultural era that followed, it was served best by loyalty to the land. In the manufacturing, industrial world it was served best by loyalty to the organisation. Today, though, that is no longer the case. Now it is served best by loyalty to the specialism, to your particular ability, to honing and shaping and moulding it to add value to others. Today, specialising, learning and deepening understanding are what make us achieve the successes we deserve.

Business today

Let's take a closer look at the most recent transition. In the Western, developed world, I would contend that the industrial age is over. Not gone, of course – it never quite will be – just as farming is not 'gone', but is no longer the primary way in which people make a living. As the industrial age diminishes, an age of mastery is replacing it. That change has an impact not just on what is done, but the reasons for it to be done at all.

No longer can the business world be divided into a definite ledger of jobs and tasks that are performed solely for money; companies' total contribution matters beyond the simple contract of value exchange with a customer. The manner in which they make their contribution also affects their value. The best companies now function with a premise of collaboration (internally, in their market, for the environment, and taking account of diversity, equity and inclusion) rather than the dog-eat-dog mentality of 'fighting' competition. The best will thrive while the rest wither and stagnate.

The work that flows from a purposeful choice for excellence will always outpace that done without passion. This new way of thinking has turned the most successful career employees away from a careerist approach. Companies have begun to adapt – first by reorganising the workspace to facilitate accommodating, as far as was possible, the personal aspirations of each employee – while ensuring that all individual purposes were aligned. The primary job of management has become the cultivation of this type of workplace, encouraging an element of individualism into the work environment.

For example, Google famously operated a culture that allowed employees to work on their own projects. Management also had to have the foresight to understand when intentions became misaligned and to nudge them back into alignment. Overall, companies have begun to focus on short-term, purposeful engagements for individual employees that allow them to build their portfolios while working toward a single goal. Businesses that allow this kind of independent collaboration and personal achievement will invariably create better work than those that do not. These companies will tend to leave the world better than they found it.

The new employee in this world will narrow their niche speciality to a sharpened point in order to be successful. For instance, an entrepreneurial investment contract lawyer will likely be much more successful than a general practice solicitor. We will discuss in the next chapter why one may choose to remain as a practitioner, probably on a good salary, while another strives to become expert or master, paid at a premium. Expertise in the new world of business places a premium on being the number one authority in a given field – the master of your art, not just another practitioner.

When companies take this strategy to heart, they will not narrow their market as they narrow their speciality; rather, they will *lead* their market because of the ability to apply a honed skill set to the problems their customers face. The question now becomes how your business moves from simply being good at what you do to being the leading authority: the only business that does precisely what you do. The answers lie in clarity of purpose, internal strategy and external implementation.

As more and more businesses do this, the world of work (and the need to employ individuals on long-term contracts) also changes. That's why the idea of a 'job for life' has been diminishing. Careers that take place within one institution or organisation have already diminished. It's still possible, but it is no longer likely. Instead, what we see are individuals opting for a 'life of jobs': being sought out because they are the perfect person to perform a specific job, and then moving on to the next gig. Many of the early adopters are now in small businesses and many of these are businesses of only one person. I think this will become more common in the future.

Does this mean larger organisations won't exist? Far from it. The word itself gives us a clue. Building a ship, designing a new computer, designing an advertising campaign and so on… these are all collective endeavours. They need a team to work together to deliver the best outcome. But does the team need to be employed by the same organisation? Of course not, it just needs to be *organised*. Excellent planning along with deeply considered strategic approaches gives a business, or the wider organisation of businesspeople, the best chance for a successful outcome.

There's a heartbeat to collective working, a rhythm beating at the core of the important work. Imagine an orchestra rehearsing and performing a piece they have not played before. Each player is a master of their instrument, but there is a conductor who provides the vision of how to interpret the piece, who shares their vision and sets the cadence with the players. Now, while each master contributes their unique talent, they bring the vision of the whole to life collectively and collaboratively. Done well, it will make your heart beat to the rhythm, and your soul will soar.

In business, to cultivate the best strategy, everyone must understand the vision and share its pace. Organisations must build collaborative teams in units that function well together. Doing so will bring clarity to all areas of focus and the vision will become a self-fulfilling prophecy. The primary function of business owners, then, is the creation of the vision, the harnessing of the right talent – their own and that of others – and the ability to create a collaborative environment in which collective endeavour can flourish.

The main challenge of this approach is in breaking the notion of exchanging time for money. The community becomes the most important aspect of the business, not anyone's individual mastery within it. People with a clear purpose (and the companies that support them) will be the catalysts of change. They will leave a legacy that will mark this period as one of the most productive in history.

Will you join this new way of working or become sidelined, slowly but surely finding your individual skill set obsolete?

Symmetry

I find a beauty in the symmetry of this change. Today's world is once again recognising the value of the human mind and its accumulated knowledge, our physical ability to develop and hone specific and valuable skills and our intellect to have the wisdom to know what really matters. Of these, it is wisdom that will always underlie the power of mastery to be building better business.

The wise

At all stages of the history that I have, rather rapidly, described here, there were individuals who had become the 'wise ones'. People who had observed well. Perhaps over time, by trial and error, or through curiosity. They are the ones we turn to when we seek certainty.

Without wise advice, building better business is simply trial and error, and the changes we try would fail often, and often badly. With wise advice there will still be failure, for different contexts have different hidden traps – but they will not fail as badly and we will know where to look for the traps. Wisdom brings with it a greater chance of building better business, and so for business owners early in their journey it makes sense to find the advisors with the wisdom you need.

In the next chapter I will explore the nature of that wisdom, how we can all work toward it, and how this gives us value wherever we are in the journey. Perhaps most importantly, we will see how mastery has a pull that continues however close to it one gets.

Being curious

Everyone knows that we continue to learn throughout our lives, yet some do stop. 'You can't teach an old dog new tricks' is often more of an excuse than an observation.

The biggest single starting point for building better business is to hone your curiosity. Look at what works for others, but before you copy it, be curious. Nothing copied works as well as something emulated because of the different contexts, subtleties and nuances.

Be curious; always ask yourself what could be better, even if what you have just achieved is the best you have ever done. Be curious too about why things work in particular ways. Try to understand nuance and uncover subtleties and experiment – perhaps especially when business is going well.

Ways to build the curiosity habit

1. Call a client and ask them an open question about their work with you. Perhaps, 'I'd like to know how our work is helping you, and how I might make it better – what are your thoughts?' Listen without interrupting, asking, 'Anything more?' when they run out.

2. Take a few minutes each day to write down what worked for you that day, what you are proud of and what you feel wasn't you at your best. Writing it down is important because it encourages you to reflect on what has happened.

3. Once a week, read back over your reflections and ask yourself if there are any common factors you can identify. Reflect on how to ensure you embed the good and improve the rest.

2 Mastery

The head alone is a tyrant. The heart alone is chaotic.
The marriage of the two is mastery.

– Carla Gordan

That special something

There are times when we meet people who have something special. It's not a single thing, and it isn't easy to describe. It is a number of elements that combine to make someone special. Their confidence and the inspiring insights in what they say, their obvious intellect (I'm referring here to their ability and willingness to think deeply rather than some arbitrary measure of intelligence) and their calmness under pressure. They show deep emotional control and an understanding of the importance of timing. We know that when they choose to speak, we'd better be listening. Somehow they know what seems to be unknowable.

In the last chapter we talked briefly about historical times, when humans gathered in tribes, roaming, hunting, gathering and setting up camp for a season, or even just a week or two. The successful would have had a wise leader – a head of the tribe who knew when to move before the food ran out or the storms came. Someone who understood the world they were in at a level others couldn't fathom. These elders or shamans were key to the tribe. They had built their understanding of the world from their own experience, and the experience and skills of those who came before them. They would have known that they also needed to develop and grow the same skills in those who were following them. They were teachers too.

Fast forward to today; there are always times when we meet someone who just knows what to do, perhaps not really understanding how. These are the people that I call 'masters'. They have mastery of their topic and themselves, and it is much more about who they are than what they do.

Meeting a master

A few years ago I had the pleasure of hearing Sir Clive Woodward tell his story of winning the Rugby World Cup with the English rugby team. When he arrived it was immediately clear that we were in for a treat. He was calm and assured. I recall the room we were in for the event was a difficult shape for a presentation, with a large number of people standing. Having scanned the room, Sir Clive selected the ideal, but not the most obvious place. He told his story (if you are interested in the whole story, I recommend his book, *Winning*) and how he brought new ideas and approaches to a game that was in the midst of turning from fundamentally amateur at its roots, to deeply professional in all the meanings of that word.[2] The audience was spellbound, and for myself, and so many others, what he achieved was not just to tell us about the joys of success on a rugby field, but how the elements could be applied in any field. I know that I felt that I had seen something very rare.

The mastery he brought was drawn not just from playing rugby (Woodward himself played most of his career at centre

---

2 Woodward, C. (2005). *Winning! The Path to Rugby World Cup Glory*. Hodder.

for Leicester) nor just from coaching (his coaching career started at London Irish and he had a spell as deputy to Andy Robinson at Bath). Yet without the knowledge of both playing and coaching, the skills honed and the experience gained over the years of both, his mastery could not have developed.

Woodward changed the status quo, as masters always do. He disrupted the way the Rugby Football Union thought about coaching. He used technology, and he selected players based not just on their performance on the pitch but their willingness to learn and change in order to improve. He used data in ways that were impossible a few years earlier, and it is interesting to note how that side of sport has developed significantly since then.

Learning

There's so much to learn from seeking to become world beating, and I could choose many other examples of people who have made a success of such ambition. I'm sure you can think of some you know, too.

There are probably similarities and consistencies between them all. Sir Clive Woodward was born without any of the knowledge he would hone later: he could not play rugby; it had to be learned, and he knew nothing of coaching. What is it that separates them from the rest of us? I'll be controversial here and suggest that it's not the skills or the experience, but the determination to make the journey to mastery, to commit to making the transitions that take people to the pinnacle of the skills they choose.

Woodward's success came from coaching, not from his skills as a player, important as those were to understanding what a coach needed to do. In sport, age tends to force retirement from the front line, and that reality pushes people to find new careers. Some will fade into obscurity, into the mass of people who just do their work. Others master their art, honing it and becoming ever more successful on an ever narrower platform, until they are not just the best at what they do, but the only person who does it. Woodward was one such person.

David Adrian Smith, who I talked about in the introduction to this book, was another. He sold his successful business to focus on some quite esoteric elements of what he did until he became the master of them. When he had achieved that, he was found by Sony Music and has produced a number of well-known album covers for globally respected bands and musicians. Today he continues to work with global brands. A tiny business in Devon, serving the world because of his mastery. We can all do this, but not all of us will choose to do what it takes.

Let's spend a little time looking at the whole journey. As you read, try to be self-critical, and see what you recognise in your own knowledge, skills and experience, and from your markets. Consider the insights that *you* have, but that *others* do not. Be prepared to be realistic, rather than optimistic, but be ready to think hard about what you need to do to move forward on this journey.

The journey

Let us explore the transitions you can make as you learn and develop a love for the work you do. I will describe the transitions from early explorer to novice, then to practitioner. These transitions must happen before others can ever recognise you as an expert and, for the very few, a master.

As a reminder of my personal journey, when I left university and walked into the offices of a small British insurance company in

London, I was – perhaps just like you when you started your first job – a little naive, but with a buzz of excitement. I knew almost nothing about insurance. I was at the very beginning of a journey toward business mastery. Over the course of 20 years I gathered the knowledge, honed my skills and experienced many setbacks and successes. That journey was to shape much of the rest of my life, just as your journey will for you, too.

The start of the journey

Looking back, I've spent time thinking about my journey and watching others. I wanted to understand how businesspeople learn, how they develop and grow and where some of the highest achievers get to on that journey.

When you began your journey you were an explorer. After listening to and observing more experienced businesspeople, those with authority, insights and knowledge, you started to try things out. Probably (if you were like me) you made lots of mistakes and, like some explorers occasionally, got lost. But if this new land was exciting enough, you continued to develop, building skills and gaining confidence as you progressed.

Study is necessary, but not sufficient on its own. Ken Pawlak and William Bergquist suggest that pedagogic learning (the same way we learn as children) is important in forming the foundations of understanding.[3] They also show that it is at this stage that many behavioural traits and habits can be formed.

We've seen this too in recent times, with businesses having to make changes in the way they work as a result of the global COVID-19 pandemic. Nearly every business had to return to explorer status for some aspects of their work, perhaps

---

3 'Four Models of Adult Education'. Available at: https://psychology.edu/about/four-models-of-adult-education, accessed 02/12/2020.

learning to use video conferencing tools or to coordinate teams now working from home.

Novices make mistakes

You can only be an explorer for a while; once you know enough to do some of the work, you start to gain experience. In this phase, you learn by trying and failing. You aren't learning by rote but through experience (something psychologist Malcolm Knowles described in 1978 as andragogic learning, or adult learning).[4] Your inexperience may trip you up, but with your knowledge, determination and intention, you will improve.

Questions are a key part of the experience, and how we all build our understanding as different tools and techniques are tried and tested. Who do we ask? Those who came before us, those who have relevant experience, honed skills and deep knowledge. Key to our own success at this stage is documenting the learning, embedding it and harnessing it. The process of learning takes time, but it is crucial in effectively moving to the next stage of development, practitioner – particularly if the ambition is to move further beyond that. Gradually, you learn how to do the best job that you can.

Professional businesses rely on practitioners

At this point in the journey, you have put the knowledge you gained from being an explorer and applied the lessons that come from the experience of your work into practice. You are

---

4 Knowles, M. S. 'Andragogy: Adult Learning Theory in Perspective'. *Community College Review* 5(3), 9–20. https://doi.org/10.1177/009155217800500302

a practitioner. For some, acquiring the skills you need can take many years. Doctors, for example, will spend six years in higher education before they begin to specialise and build experience in the area they choose. Similarly, airline pilots spend many years learning to fly, first in small planes and then in simulators. Only then can they have some time at the controls of a large passenger flight.

All the learning is put into practice as you become a solid, capable business practitioner who works effectively and efficiently. *The journey to mastery takes time.* If you want to be a professional you need to dedicate the time it takes, to be the explorer, to move on to being a novice and then to become a practitioner. *There are no shortcuts on the journey to mastery.* All of the knowledge and the time to hone the skills and gather the experience are essential to building expertise.

For many practitioners this is where they choose, consciously or not, to stop their journey. They are capable and competent in their work and use work as a means to support other activities. Perhaps they will pursue mastery in those different crafts or in hobbies.

Stepping up by building expertise

For some, further development is not a goal. Being good at what they do is sufficient, and they choose to remain as accomplished practitioners in their field. Is that you, or do you want to push on?

Most businesses perform well at what they do because they have great practitioners delivering the work. To build expertise and become recognised as an expert you have to share your knowledge. As a practitioner, you probably taught the explorers and novices what they needed to know to do the work. That teaching helped you to understand your work in more depth – not just the way to do it, but as you start to recognise the nuances and subtleties you begin to stand out. Others see you as an expert in your field. You are getting to the top of your game.

When I see people here, I've noticed how their work changes with leadership of others. They spend less time with the explorers and novices, and more with practitioners, and even those who are becoming expert themselves. The psychologists tell us that this is now about transformative education: passing on your understanding of the nature of what you do, rather than just how you do it. Experts know how to take experience in one context and apply it in another.

Too often I have seen businesspeople race to take leadership roles, but if you move too quickly you may not have the tools you need to be an expert. Without them, you simply cannot reach mastery. *In the journey to mastery, you can only move on when you are truly ready.*

When you push ahead without the foundations of the previous steps, you will find times when you are out of your depth, feeling like an imposter and without the confidence to harness your true value to others.

Taking better photographs (or being a better photographer)

Recently I took a Masterclass course in photography. Photography has been a hobby of mine for some time. I would say that I am reasonably good at handling a camera. A solid practitioner, with some expertise, but not yet quite ready to be considered an expert. The course I studied was from Jimmy

Chin, an adventure photographer working with magazines like *National Geographic*. While his course did not directly teach me to take better photographs, it did teach me what it would mean to be a photographer; that an emphasis on who I am, my identity, rather than my skill, is an important focus.

I see a similar differentiation with the people I work with when, as experts in their field, they seek to raise their game further. To do that they have to think about how they turn up in the world, how they behave and how they address issues in their field. Lifting your game means asking the questions that few ask, and that is a special skill. Is it a skill you have honed yet?

The pinnacle of mastery

For a very few, the call to mastery remains powerful and compelling. They start to think about their identity rather than their profession. They appreciate all that they know, and their skills at a deep level – indeed, they learn what it means to truly appreciate all that has gone before and how it has created the person they now are. From a psychological viewpoint, this time of learning is qualitatively different from the others. Known as appreciative learning, it is emotional and difficult, but it is critical if you wish to become a master. As a master you will advise and counsel rather than direct, and you will be able, in an instant, to lift the conversation to a higher level. You will help people to *be*, rather than to *do*. 'Master' is a role, not a title; it is borne of action and values, not self-proclamation or accreditation. It's not about self or ego, but the greater good of the greatest number of people. Your wisdom will be sought widely and respected by all.

For many people, that depth of understanding of what they do, mastery of it, is simply not required. As practitioners and experts, their work provides all that they need. Only a few will decide to climb to this higher pinnacle. That said, if you are involved in the running of a business, making all the strategic decisions, and want the business to be recognised as exceptional at what it does so that people seek you out, then mastery is one way, perhaps the only way, to achieve that.

What you inspect

I've identified that the journey to mastery is not quick. In fact, in some areas it is a journey for which one lifetime alone may not be long enough. For example, Darwin's work mastered one aspect of how natural selection plays its part in the development of species. It was an area which, at the time, was seen as unconventional, perhaps even heretical, but it paved the way for others to look at aspects of his knowledge and take it further. Darwin's mastery of natural selection led to an understanding of the mechanism of passing on traits through genetics. Watson, Crick, Wilkins and Franklin were able to understand the mechanism of that – DNA – and, from their work, ultimately, the world now has masters in genetics whose deep insights helped to create vaccines for the coronavirus.

Like so many journeys, there's much to see, to excite, to motivate, and to learn along the way. All of which requires determination and focus. Like every journey worth undertaking, the journey to mastery will lift you from the first step.

For the few, not the many

I've identified that only a few will have the commitment to complete the journey to mastery. There, they elevate others in their market, and the market itself. This isn't because only a few can be chosen. It's because only a few will choose to make that journey their life's work.

To make that choice requires a willingness to change. It's this reality that stops many from making the transition. Why? Because to do so means letting go of much of the *doing* in favour of *being*. It's a hard choice. For many, letting go of often very hard-won skills in favour of supporting others to do the same work (and, perhaps, take it further) is tough. You can't complete the journey to mastery without the skills or the experience. They are necessary, but not sufficient.

In essence, then, mastery is about mindset and identity more than capability, skills or knowledge. It's important to focus on understanding your place in the work you do – your identity.

Pride

Pride can get in the way of this change. Pride in the work you do so well, pride in the value that you add as a practitioner of your art or the pride that comes from the recognition, by others, of your expertise. You have to let it go.

Your motivation, your pride and your joy have to shift from your own achievements to the achievements of others. Do that in the knowledge of your influence on their capability. You will no longer lift the trophy. That's for them, and you make it possible for many more to do so while you will stand back, away from the limelight.

This requires you to be humble, never to brag and to be a rock for the people you care about. Always there, always supportive, always guiding – never judging.

In all my years of work, nobody I have seen has made this change seamlessly. Everyone falters at the boundary; they doubt their right to step up. If your imposter voice is screaming at you that you are not worthy, not capable, and not ready, and yet in the quiet moments you know, for sure, that you are – then take the step.

Steps on the journey to mastery

Watching my clients over many years, I have observed some common factors.

Powerful and universal among these is a willingness to seek out stillness, perhaps through meditation, walking alone, reflection, silence or some other form of powerful relaxation. I believe that, in order to free the mind, one also has to create the space for it to be still.

Also universal is a determination to think deeply, perhaps with a Thinking Partner, which has much to recommend it. Thinking Partners are a result of the work of Nancy Kline, and a powerful way to be given the gift of space by a partner in an environment created to allow depth of thought and reflection. In this time you are guaranteed the opportunity to allow your thoughts their full expanse. It is extraordinary what can happen when you are honoured by the gift of appreciative attention without interruption. It is in these times that I have faced the things that needed to change and unlocked the subtleties and nuances of my work. You will too. Having freed the mind, this approach can turn its capacity to a more focused effort, unlocking insight after insight as you open your mind to all that is possible.[5]

While not universal in the chosen approach, there are always people involved in the transition to mastery: advisors, sounding boards, mastery group members, other experts, teachers, guides and coaches. Nobody makes this transition without the insight and support of others.

---

5 Kline, N. (2015). *More Time to Think: The Power of Independent Thinking*. Cassell.

Why are these three important? I think because this transition is about your character. Unless you know yourself, you will not become a master of your art, however hard you strive. In getting to know yourself, you will have to change. I can assure you that the changes you make, however subtle, will make you wish you had done so years before!

Responsibilities and rewards

As we journey to mastery we are faced with many responsibilities and reap many rewards. When we are explorers and novices we look to the practitioners and experts to help us. Practitioners are often also great teachers, but their relative inexperience means they can only charge basic rates, if they can charge at all, for their support. Experts tend to work with those who are practitioners, lifting their skills, and they charge a premium rate for that work. The masters, though, are revered and spend their time working, generally, with those who are already established practitioners and experts charging the highest rates.

I recall one of my mentors – an executive in one of the UK's major banks – who was at the top of his game. He was recognised by the regulators, by government and by peers as one of the foremost experts in his market. He was supported by someone whose mastery of one small aspect of his skills made their fee of thousands of pounds an hour worth every penny to him.

Those who seek out a master's wisdom care about the value of the work. The costs are almost irrelevant because the value is so great, and the fees reflect that reality.

Pricing value

In a recent search for negotiation skills training, for example, I found a number of courses starting from $30/£20 online for about 30 hours of video-based training. I could find pretty much any price – including a fee of $7,000 from the former FBI negotiation expert, Chris Voss. That fee was for just a few hours' work in a small group setting. Chris wasn't training; he was critiquing, providing opportunities to role play, test and extend existing skills. That's a technique that masters use to lift the already expert performance of others.

For anyone starting out in negotiation, Chris Voss's course might help a bit, yet many of the subtleties would be missed. For an already experienced negotiator, it will encourage them to work on their skills and give insights on where there were weaknesses. Yet, for an expert negotiator, it would be transformative. This has appreciative learning at its heart: each critique gives voice to the wisdom that is unlocked by the tutor and exposed to the student.[6]

If you are already an expert in what you do, I hope you charge the appropriate fee for your level of expertise. Playing small, sharing practitioner insights to help novices for the few pounds they can afford, keeps you small. Playing small will hold you back from becoming the master you want to be. All too often I see businesses failing to reach their potential because they undersell their skills. Even in difficult times, don't let that be you.

---

6 'Four Models of Adult Education'. Available at: https://psychology.edu/about/four-models-of-adult-education, accessed 02/12/2020.

Stay fresh, stay connected

I said earlier that to reach mastery one had to let go of doing the work. practitioners and experts do that, yet masters must not become completely divorced from their art; they still do the work as well, but only for some of the time, perhaps quite a small part of it. Without that connection to their roots, much would wither quickly on the vine. Mastery is not a fixed state, but a dynamic one.

For masters of their art, understanding how the world is changing over time is important. The work is always evolving, as others build their understanding and add to knowledge. One of the great underlying skills of masters is the ability to see what will happen in a different context. This ability to accurately assess how often small and nuanced differences will change the outcome of a set of actions is a superpower. In my work I've seen businesses rush to emulate successes they see elsewhere in their market, only for it to come up short when they do. There are always differences, but can you tell which ones matter and which can be ignored? Masters can.

Time to inspect

Another of my past mentors, Des Robertson, said, 'You do not get what you expect; you get what you inspect!' This was a master who understood that you have to keep your hand in the market in which you work. You have to keep watching because it is changing every day. One of the best ways to watch is to do.

Gravity

Masters do something special with the expertise they have built up. They model it. They build an understanding of their world by creating a descriptive model that explains it in simpler terms. Sometimes this is about underpinning a theory, providing a detailed understanding of the way that something appears in our world. Sometimes it's overarching, bringing the disparate together into a coherent whole. Always, it's about extracting from an understanding of what happens in specific situations to what can be generally understood.

Albert Einstein brought together an overarching theory of how space and time work together. He created a model he called spacetime, and the theory was called the special theory of relativity. It was an overarching theory that allowed him to examine space and time in new ways. Those new ways give better insights into how our physical world works.

He didn't stop there. His thinking continued and led him to develop an underpinning theory. A few years later, he formalised this thinking in the general theory of relativity, which described how gravity might work. That theory suggested that there may be particles or waves that transmit gravity over long distances. The particles are called gravitons. At the time of writing, the existence of the graviton remains unsubstantiated, but in a large step toward that proof, the 2017 Nobel Prize for Physics was awarded for work on demonstrating gravitational waves that were consistent with the theory.[7]

---

7 'The Nobel Prize in Physics 2017'. Available at: https://www.nobelprize.org/prizes/physics/2017/summary, accessed 23/08/2021.

Einstein was brilliant, a master of thinking about the physical world, but it was his new insights and unique perspective that stood him apart.

When we look at business, we can also see a few people who have done the same, who have the same exceptional insights and thinking to set them apart. A scan of the business section of the papers will highlight those who are masters.

Unique and inspiring

The journey to mastery is characterised by explorers seeking knowledge, novices seeking experience, practitioners seeking understanding and experts seeking wisdom. Mastery is not *the* destination, rather it is the start of a period, perhaps a lifetime, of enhancing and honing wisdom. Masters are looking at different contexts and seeking new insights from what is learned. They are seeking enlightenment.

Mastery is a state of self-awareness, a deepening of one's knowledge, not just of what you do but of yourself. It comes with a determination to address and improve those areas of yourself which do not currently serve you. It is no surprise to me that meditation, silence, thinking and a calm, reassured maturity tend to be present in those who have attained mastery. When you meet a master from whom you seek advice, you know you are in the presence of great wisdom. They unerringly, yet consistently, ask questions that have a laser-like focus. As a side note, masters tend to ask questions of those who seek their insights, guiding them to the same understanding rather than giving answers. They illuminate, through those questions, without judgement. When they listen, they do so with a quality that few ever manage. They say just a few words, to which we must listen well, and reflect upon before jumping to conclusions. Their words have a power and insight that general advice can never match.

For you, as you approach mastery, it is important to recognise the power and importance your mastery has – not just for you, but for all the people you reach, directly and indirectly. Your words, insights, analysis, skill, experience and knowledge combine in ways few others can bring to bear.

This is who you have become: the unique, inspiring person you were always meant to be.

A note on imposter syndrome

Not everything that is faced can be changed. But nothing can be changed until it is faced.

– James Baldwin

Out of our depth

We all feel, from time to time, a little bit out of our depth. Imposter syndrome is a pattern in which someone doubts their skills, talents or accomplishments and is often expressed as a concern of being seen as a fraud. It is my opinion that these emotions are actually a strength, even though our internal voice wants to convince us of some personal weakness.

The first time I am asked to do anything new, whether that's a new activity or a familiar one in a new context, my mind always asks me, 'Can you?' How can I possibly know *precisely* what to do? For example, the first time I was asked to take a less experienced diver with me underwater and become responsible for his safety, did I feel ready? When I asked myself to write this book, did I know what it would actually involve? All these times, did the voice in my head tell me I was ready and capable or did it warn me to be careful?

How could you use those moments?

What is really happening is that, in the nearest equivalent role, we understand that our knowledge and experience has made us competent practitioners, experts, perhaps even masters. Yet, in this new context we are having to step back to an earlier stage. Perhaps it is something we have no experience of, so we need to be explorers. More likely it is just that we are asking ourselves to step back a stage or two. In doing so, we recall how we felt about the mistakes we've made. The memory of that feeling feeds the voice we hear. Yet it also tells us what we need to do.

When I was asked to take my first novice diver into a long, relatively deep dive, I knew his life depended on me. I could not make mistakes – the consequences would be massive. I was, by this point, a competent, even expert, diver. I had trained and qualified as an instructor and had been coaching and training novices in swimming pools and shallow, non-tidal waters. This was a different moment. At best, I was being asked to look after another diver's safety as a practitioner, in the context of the planned depth and the tidal currents we would face. I looked around the boat. Calmly getting ready for the day was Steve, a deeply experienced professional diver with thousands of hours underwater to his name. He and I had dived together for some time with me as his protégé. I asked him what I might forget and what I must remember in the role I was about to undertake. He smiled, laughed, and told me three or four things that I knew but had not given the right importance to. He concluded by saying, '... and you'll do a great job because you know that you needed to ask. The people who don't ask screw up; the ones who ask rarely do. Have a great dive!' We did. Yet on reflection, there were myriad elements to learn – all of which helped accelerate my expertise in that role, too.

Imposter syndrome is little more than a reminder to understand where we are (perhaps also who we are), in the context of the task at hand, on our journey to mastery or, more to the point, where we are choosing to put ourselves.

A moment of reflection when we hear that voice of concern can lead us to recognise the stage we are stepping back to. (Of course, it may be that the reflection stops us making a mistake.) Are we being asked to do something we know nothing about (like an explorer), or to do something where we know the basics but have little experience (like a novice)? Perhaps we are being asked to do something we haven't done for a while, but were good at in the past (like a practitioner). This tells us how we need to deal with the challenge, and the type of learning we need.

My imposter voice told me I didn't know enough to make the dive as safe as it could be, but I knew I was already doing a good job at protecting novice divers in other places. My conversation with a more experienced and expert dive leader enabled me to draw on his experience. We had a really enjoyable dive as a result of that small check-in. The experience, and my reflections afterwards, helped to lift my game further.

So, for me, I've always welcomed that moment of doubt, the imposter syndrome warning voice, as it tells me that I am at the edge of my experience, and that whatever happens next, if I am alert, there will be learning. It tells me to step forward and to be observant. That pause also gives me space to determine precisely what I need to do next to do the job at hand to the very best of my ability. In many ways, this is a superpower.

Preparing for mastery

We know now that mastery is a journey, and an enduring one. As you choose to make that journey it is important that you take time to consider what you wish to master. The first step is to become not just an expert in the skills you choose, but *the* expert, and only then will you be ready to move on. Do not worry at this stage if what really excites you is something you know little about yet, as every master was an explorer once.

Ways to prepare for mastery

1. Take some time to reflect on the work you do, and decide which parts of it matter most to you.

2. Listen to what others tell you about your skills in those areas and think about 'your way' of delivering your work. How is it different from others in the market?

3. Decide which parts of what you do you wish to work on. How will you deepen your experience, expand your knowledge and hone your skills? Which part will you consider mastering?

---

3 Better on Purpose

Whatever you can do, or dream you can, begin it.
Boldness has genius, power, and magic in it.

– Quoted by W. H. Murray, in *The Scottish Himalayan Expedition*, from
a loose translation of Goethe's *Faust* made by John Anster in 1835.[8]

Different meaning, same word

As I mentioned in the introduction 'better' is one of those words that can take many different meanings, depending on your context and your current situation. Over the years I've discussed with many business owners and leaders what would be 'better' for them. For some, it means greater revenues, perhaps for personal financial reasons or as part of a larger growth strategy. Related to that, for some better is about employing more people and having greater presence in their market. Better might be about reputation, particularly if a historic incident has dented the view people have of your business. For some, it was more about gathering some time back for other activities in their lives; a better business was one that still did everything it was doing but needed less of

---

8 'W. H. Murray'. Available at: https://en.wikipedia.org/wiki/W._H._Murray, accessed 19/02/2021.

the owner's time. For many, the key driver of better was the impact the business was having on their levels of stress, their emotions, feelings, relationships and family. Better meant something to do with control.

Also, we are building 'better', not 'best' – that might sound like it's aiming for something less than we could, but I think the opposite is true. What is better changes and evolves. What is best today may simply be ordinary in a year or two, forgotten in a decade. As you read this book, I encourage you to think with an open mind, knowing that you are setting the direction of your business to improve it, with a strategic aim, and a determination to keep building and evolving where the end state will be.

No two businesses are identical, and yet, far more often than not, what's better for the business is better for the business owner too. Better is a personal decision. Understanding and visualising what would be better for you provides insights into your intentions for the business.

Building better business is really about a way of being, and to achieve that consistently and reliably you will have to become the master of your art. To reach that mastery, you might also have to take some of the things that you do apart, discarding, dismantling or demolishing them in favour of a better way. Those parts which do not support you, even if you enjoy them, have to go because one aspect of a better business is that there is much joy and laughter in it. You will have, if you decide to travel, a remarkable and deeply enlightening journey.

The building and rebuilding of walls

One hundred and eleven years ago, someone lifted a block of rough-hewn limestone from the new quarry near Wintour's Leap outside Chepstow. They carried it just a few yards to build it into a garden wall using lime mortar to secure it in place. At about the same time, whoever was working on that wall drank a mug of Bovril, discarding the now empty jar into the space between the two skins of the wall. In my mind's eye, I see a chilly autumn day, and a builder with cold and sore hands wrapped around a steaming mug enjoying the flavour and savouring his work.

One hundred and eleven years later, ivy cascaded over a now rather sad and neglected wall. I snipped through the final thick stem, and about two metres of wall tumbled at my feet. Most of that old lime mortar now crumbled to dust. The limestone blocks fell onto Offa's Dyke Path (more an ancient administrative border between England and Wales than a formal dyke), which runs alongside our wall. In the rubble, exposed, undamaged, the discarded Bovril bottle. A hand-blown brown bottle moulded with the brand name visible, yet instantly recognisable by its shape, even today.

I cleared and stacked the stones. I dismantled until I found solid foundations, good footings. I was ready to start the rebuilding work. I mixed up some new lime mortar and selected the best stones. I laid three courses of stones on each side of the wall that was damaged. It was not finished, but it was already taking shape.

As I worked, a family walked down the path. The younger man paused. He commented that I had demolished a lot. 'Could it not have been patched?' he asked.

Before I could reply, his father said, 'Son, if you want to do a better job sometimes you have to take things back to the foundations, start again, and build it stronger.'

I smiled as they continued their walk.

Building business

We can all build processes on top of the old method. Have you designed systems and then adapted them? Changed the parts that do not work as you intended them to? Have you added another patch? Another bit of extra glue? Or do you cut the last tie to the way it has been done and build afresh?

So often it's not simply a choice between rebuilding something as it was or starting completely from scratch. The house and garden were built on a hill. There was a strong slope in the garden and the existing wall followed it. When we moved in, we'd done a lot of work to terrace the garden, and when the wall needed rebuilding, I redesigned it to follow the terraces. We decided we would add a fence above the wall, and changed the design to include fence posts built into it.

In business too, whenever there is change, rebuilding or building from scratch, there is an opportunity for new, intentional, purposeful design. That chance should always be considered and taken if needed. What will happen if we reconsider how we do what we do, and make it better? If you trust yourself to create a better outcome, you *will* make that choice. So, if you do not make those choices often enough, then ask what you would need to do to have more trust in yourself.

Better business

I have had to take the wall apart in order to rebuild it better with a new design. It is still on the old foundations – there's nothing wrong with them. I now have a wall that will last at least another century.

If you look at your business and identify aspects that need to change, then, if you change them, you can have a business that is reliable, consistent and strong. So, be bold and take apart those parts of your business that no longer support you. Rebuild them. Design them differently, intentionally, with care and precision and strategy at the heart of what you do.

There's something else here too. If I'd got to work on improving the wall too early, I wouldn't have seen the weak spots that had not yet broken. Too late and I would have been firefighting – it would have taken too long to fix some aspects that were beyond the pale. The ideal is to be making a change when the weaknesses are seen, but before they are critical. When that is done well, the changes may not take much effort, but have a big impact and endure for a long time. Those tests, both of what has to change and how enduring the replacement will be, are at the heart of building better business.

But let's go a bit further. There are some things about an ancient crumbling wall that are obvious: it doesn't have the strength that it once had, and while it may not yet have *failed*, it is *failing*. All change requires us to recognise that there is an element of failing involved. This is, in part, why change is so hard. If our business process has worked well in the past, but the needs of clients have changed, then despite all that we have invested in the process, it remains one that is failing. For so many, failure is an evocative word that can block and challenge their identity. Logically, if a business process needs to change, nobody has failed – yet it often feels like a personal failure at an emotional level. In a later chapter I will discuss the power that emotions and feelings can have over our ability to be building better business, but for now let's just hold the thought that there is an impact.

Change, however it feels, driven by necessity, or a desire to improve, is always an opportunity to design the better business you seek with intention and with purpose. In your business too, you can evolve what you are working on as new information becomes available. Better isn't a static thing, but a dynamic one, and as you continue to do the work it becomes impossible not to change if you see something even better.

Boundaries

There are risks with an approach that encourages evolutionary change as you go. If you constantly change direction, it is confusing both for you as the business owner and for your clients and suppliers. My garden wall continues to follow the old foundations and stays at the boundary. I know what the limitations are as well as the freedom to work in a different style or with a subtle change in shape.

This is true in business too. We aren't constrained by changing details that *improve* the outcome, but we should be much more cautious about changing those that *replace* the outcome with something unrecognisable. Building better business is a strategic approach. The strategy is visualised by defining what better means. For those changes, we need to think strategically.

Thinking strategically can sound grand, but really it just means only reacting to the current situation by considering the future situation you are aiming for, and not (just) the immediate impact of what is happening now. Your earlier visualisation of what 'better' meant to you provides the insights to do that well. The first step is to check that your original intention remains valid, the second is to determine if what you are doing, or thinking of doing, moves you toward that, or not. For the garden wall, the change we made to add a gateway didn't change the longer-term ambition of a better boundary running along the original foundations – in fact, it enhanced it.

There's something more powerful here though. By creating boundaries, effectively decision constraints, we actually create the freedom to express ourselves better within them. That means, perhaps, that we can focus our best work on the clients who need and want it and avoid attracting clients for whom we are not a good fit. Perhaps it means we know how to choose where to invest in our personal development, or in better infrastructure for the business going forward.

The most important aspect of this is to be clear about your boundaries, and one way to identify them is to think about what cannot change, or what, if it did change, would make things worse. Creating a written or visual description of the business – not just of what you want it to be, but also what you don't want it to become – can help guide your decision making in the immediate future, too.

Not having boundaries may sound liberating, but in reality we lose context, and without context, decision making is likely to be more random and much less effective. Boundaries give you freedom within them – freedom to make better choices.

Context, feel and experience

Every skilled task has a multitude of subtle aspects that the explorers, novices and even early practitioners will miss. When I first started building the wall, I'd mix up a batch of lime mortar by careful measurement of the components of sand, lime and water. Initially, I didn't know what consistency the mix should have, I couldn't tell from the resistance it put up to a trowel whether it was strong enough to build with, yet wet enough to flow just the right amount into the surface imperfections of the stone. Too wet and the stones' weight would cause it to flow out of the joint. Too dry and the bond wouldn't bite.

Yet, over time and experience that transition from novice to practitioner took place. Today I mix the mortar by feel and touch, and I can create a mortar that works well, that is structurally strong even when first mixed, and which creates a strong lasting bond. It's workable for several hours, but it changes over that time, and there's an optimum moment to brush out excess from the joints to create a clean and sharp look to the finished build.

A master builder goes further. Their experience allows them to tell a novice how to 'feel' the differences I've described. They can offer their guidance while a novice works, inviting them to consider how resistive the mix is to a trowel and to its edge. How the mortar sticks to the trowel and how well it holds its shape. They know the colour it should be, and they know how it changes as external properties like the temperature, brightness or humidity of the day change. A master builder training a novice will invite them to explore these experiences, guiding them to understand how the best results feel, look and smell. They let the novice understand their touch and gradually the skill develops. The master knows that they've gone back to foundations and built a strong and lasting legacy of skill in them too. And when they do that, there's a smile and a satisfaction that goes far beyond their own work. A master builder may build a thousand walls themselves, but through their mastery a million more will come to pass.

In all of this work our experience continues to grow, and the wise, the masters (see Chapter 2), use that experience to uncover insight, and to reflect, review and redefine what they are doing. What they also do is look forward to the vision of the better business that they want to build. They hone the skills they need over time. thinking strategically about the intention of a better business.

There's something else too. This isn't just about a focus on the business – it's important to spend time to make sure that you also consider yourself. As Stephen Covey reminds us in *The Seven Habits of Highly Effective People*, it is important to 'sharpen the saw' – and when it comes to being a business owner, you are the saw![9]

If we consider top-level sport, some achieve greatness on the field, but when that career is over, few go on to coach others. That's partly because it requires mastery to be able to pass on practical skills to others, to lift them to greater success. Often, it's not the very best at doing something who go on to become masters, but those whose experience uncovered insights that others need to accelerate their journey.

The impact of those insights is powerfully enduring because the masters pass them on to others on the journey. They last long after the master's involvement; the greatest wisdom shapes and changes generations. It is a legacy for good.

---

9 Covey, S. R. (2004). *Seven Habits of Highly Effective People*. Simon & Schuster UK.

A focus on forever

The legacy of mastery

Let's explore that concept of leaving a legacy. Many talk about 'legacy', and for some the things that will outlast our own short lives are obvious. When we think about some of the people who have left an enduring mark on the world, there are things that become obvious. Anything that is physically built to last, will last, but the people or person who built it will usually be long forgotten in the mists of time. Do you, for example, know the names of the people who built your house? Occasionally people are remembered for their ideas, but not often.

A few, a very few, stay with us, effectively, forever. Hadrian is known for building a wall; Knut for not understanding tides; Einstein will remain famous; Neil Armstrong will always have taken a small step. The reality is that the sort of universal enduring awareness of our existence is not a legacy very many of the people alive today will leave.

Yet there is the opportunity for legacy for and from all of us. It appears in many forms and endures for different reasons. Our children take our influence with them, but in business our clients, suppliers, staff and markets are all influenced by what we do as individuals, mostly by how we turn up, by who we are.

Mastery leaves a legacy, *always*. All the people influenced, supported, lifted and encouraged by the work done are changed. Your mastery spreads to experts, practitioners, novices and explorers. One action has many consequences, and that is why we must use it wisely. That it was you, that your name is associated with it, is unlikely; that your mastery endures is a certainty.

Starting work

More than 40 years ago, as a young St Andrew's graduate, I sat down in an office on the 7th floor of a building that ran between Mincing Lane and Mark Lane in the City. My boss, and later mentor, Bill, sucked quietly on his pipe and blew thoughtful clouds of smoke that drifted throughout the office. He explained the traditions of an industry that had started in a coffee shop a few streets away. On that day he kicked the young graduate's career off. Over the coming months and years I realised how much the older one knew. Yet mostly the older man listened, so that he could offer a nudge in the right direction when it was needed. In the privilege of all privileges he knew when to let things play out, because the value of the learning was more than the cost of the mistake being made. He taught the value of understanding the context of risk, of opportunity, of the joy of learning and the importance of giving.

Bill was an advocate of trial and error, but not in the unstructured way that most understand it. For him the purpose of trial and error was to learn. He used to say 'errors are a natural part of work, an opportunity to learn, and change, and grow. The only real error is to repeat the avoidable ones.' He would discuss with me, his mentee, how I might improve the way I did business. As a novice, my ideas were most often flawed because they lacked a nugget of information that experience would bring. But a novice also carries very little baggage. They don't know 'the way we do things here', so they cannot be constrained by them. Haven't we all experienced trying something that doesn't work only to return to it later, when other elements have changed, to find that it can - now - succeed?

For example, in the early days of the internet, a video could take hours to film, render and upload. For many viewers, buffering was a constant companion. The experience was poor. Today, we do video on the fly, streaming to the internet and being watched almost live – sometimes by massive audiences. Some of the early users of video still cite the problems they faced as reasons not to adopt it today.

Over the years, much of the physical environment where I learned my trade has changed. The office building has been demolished; it's now the London Underwriting Centre. The company was bought and sold and merged into others, existing now only as a specialist musical instrument insurance brand. Bill, long since retired, knows that he guided and advised his many mentees for many years until they too could support and guide others in their turn.

Of course, I always remember that first conversation as the start of a journey, the business lessons I can now enjoy passing on in the mentoring work I do, and in this book. It is a journey on which I continue to travel.

Learning by doing

Bill was already a master when I first met him, and his thinking and guidance still drive my hand today. In turn, I hope that my work will have lifted others in similar ways. This isn't really about passing on knowledge, although in our explorer phase that is what we crave. It's much more about the mindset of someone who has reached what we aspire to become.

When businesses become successful, it becomes common to ask about the choices those companies would make. I've heard this about Google ('What would Google do?'), Virgin, Amazon and many others over the years. It is because they approach business with an innovative product or a different mindset, and business leaders ask themselves what they need to learn from it. When the wiser ones do that, they aren't seeking knowledge from another business's experience; they are seeking insight from it – wisdom. They seek to understand the concepts and the context, and then aim to apply it in a different context; their own.

What I learned from Bill, bearing in mind that we were, at the time, working for a minnow in a pond of very big fish, was that it's not always possible to do exactly what the bigger fish do. Some of their activity is resource intensive, and as a smaller business, matching their spending or committing the time or resources needed can be effectively impossible. Yet, it is always possible, although sometimes not easy, to see why what they did worked in their markets. Bill said, 'It's not "how" they do it that matters, but understanding what they were really trying to achieve, what made that important and why it was purposeful.' A major competitor had achieved significant market share in a specialist insurance product. It was important because it gave them economies of scale, but it aligned with the ethos of that business to be focused on a specialism and be the go-to insurer for people who needed that cover.

It was no surprise to me that the business Bill and I worked for was ultimately sold, long after our time with it. It was merged into one of the bigger insurers and effectively disappeared. Yet its prime specialism, musical instruments insurance, still bears the company branding to this day.[10]

I recall one aspect of what we talked about then was how some of the products that really worked only became popular after a lot of mistakes and attempts had been tried. It's reported that Dyson had some 15 years and over 5,000 prototypes before the first bagless machine went to market.[11] None of us

---

10 'British Reserve Insurance Co Ltd – Company Profile and News', Bloomberg Markets. Available at: www.bloomberg.com/profile/company/1769Z:LN, accessed 08/02/2021.
11 'It Took James Dyson 15 Years to Make a Bagless Vacuum'. Available at: www.inc. com/ilan-mochari/vacuum-innovation.html, accessed 08/02/2021.

saw any of that – we only saw the end product. Yet the obvious truth is that, however small you are, you have to try things and they won't all work. The question James Dyson asked of each prototype was, 'Is this better?'

Amazon is another example, having grown today to the global force that they have become. When the founder, Jeff Bezos, was asked what lies behind the success, he said: 'If there's one reason we have done better than our peers in the internet space over the last six years, it is because we have focused like a laser on customer experience.'

Again, whatever size of business you run, this is something we can all apply. Whether you are a business that provides a product and has no direct contact with its end consumers, or a service business that interacts at every point of the service with its clients, your customers define your business success. Amazon's focus hasn't meant a bland, beige, acceptable-to-everyone customer interface. They do not seek to support every customer in every possible way. What they have done is optimise, test and evolve. The question they continually ask is 'Is this better?' Where the answer is yes, the change is retained.

Better business is consistent and enduring, and when we intentionally create new and better ways of working, they will endure.

Amazon's done something else too. In order to make things better, as observed through the lens of the implementation of conscious decisions of the Amazon leadership with the assumed intention of improving the business: they have built global infrastructure – servers, databases, search algorithms, web design and more. All of that was needed to meet their goals at the time they were introduced. Jeff Bezos's vision changed as the business grew, and it continues to evolve today. Initially focused on disrupting the book market, the company had created the opportunity for other goods to be sold through the same process. Once the distribution network was established and there was sufficient volume it was possible to deliver perishables. That needed extensive information technology and the capacity to handle the volume of traffic.

Those things have a side effect. In order to have enough server capacity they had to have more than they needed except for the highest of the highest peak times. Mostly that means they have under-utilised resources. For Jeff Bezos's team that is anathema. Amazon Web Services (AWS) was born. If you need a powerful server for a few minutes, rent it from AWS – it costs a few cents. Need massive amounts of data stored offsite? Use AWS. Need to send large volumes of email? Use AWS.

Amazon, particularly AWS, provides the infrastructure for much of the business IT and is used by many businesses, large and small, including mine. Did those early designers and coders have my use-case in mind when they did their work? Of course not. What they did was create something and then offer it to the market. As people found uses, they evolved what they had done to add more value, but their approach was not one of control; it was one of observation and improvement while ensuring that their internal 'better' was either enhanced or unaffected.

You can't control how others use what you give them. But you can learn from what others do to keep building on what you have already got.

Yet who coded the software? Who designed the hardware configurations? Who is working on it today? Few know, yet their work endures, and the principles they have developed are being applied in many other contexts by many other businesses. As others start being influenced by what has been built, the value becomes clearer. While Amazon built AWS to support its own business, they have also seen how others use the tools they needed. That knowledge helps Amazon too, and new and different ways to create and take advantage of the value being created emerge, which now loop back into Amazon's model. That, of course, locks in the approach, at least until an even better way emerges.

In other words, making the value clear ensures that the value remains. Clarity comes from seeing how the ideas, products and services are really applied, and understanding what that has brought to those who use them.

Measurements, interim steps and reflection

Building better business is, in part at least, about looking at how one can improve the processes the business employs. It doesn't mean looking at a long-term goal and waiting to secure everything you will need for that goal to be realised before making a change now. Most likely, you will build structures and processes that are needed to get you to your goal but will be discarded once you are there. For an arch, scaffolding is only needed to support the stones until you can add the keystone (which creates the arch's strength). Then the scaffolding can be removed. This is true in business too. In order to be building better business there are times when work is done that will later be undone on the road to the goal. For example, a growing business may use shared workplaces as an interim step to opening its own office.

Our long-term ambitions are often, not always, about creating and building better so that the changes we make can be enduring. If your ambitions don't feel like they are anything more than a milestone on a journey with an as-yet-undefined destination, I would invite you to think more. Having a focus on forever has really helped me to consider what it is that I want to deliver so that my work changes things – not just for my clients, but for others too, and not just in my lifetime, but in an enduring way. Thinking hard about what makes mastery something to shoot for has given me the inspiration to take the thinking to as many people as I can. This book is one example of how that can be done.

That focus doesn't always tell me what to do today, to move me forward. That's a challenge that as businesspeople we also need to address. Working backwards, I ask, 'What does that big and bold ambition mean I need to be able to do by the end of this year, this quarter and this month?'

Remembering Bill's advice of conscious, purposeful trial-and-error, it's OK not to be certain if what is done will work and will move you on the right road. Yet it is important to understand what you're trialling, why you're trialling it and how you expect it to work (and how it might fail). What you must do is to be clear how that trial will be measured, and you must measure it. It never ceases to amaze me how often people identify measures for work they are doing, but then never actually record the measures. With the data you can reflect, review and redefine your ambitions, and better understand what you now need to (try to) do. For me, this is where working with a mentor or an accountability partner or group is so vital.

Mastery is a long-term aspiration

I chose the title of this chapter with the intention of thinking in the very, very long term. I have heard that some cultures, particularly in the East, naturally think in that way, designing what they plan for great-great-grandchildren whose existence may not ever come to pass. Any business may not survive, and few, perhaps none, survive unchanged. That reality raises the question of whether such long-term planning has any value at all. It is, after all, little more than an aspiration – a fictional ambition. But such long-term thinking has an impact on current activity. It's not hypothetical after all, but an arrow, a signpost. As we shall see later in Chapter 9, a good signpost doesn't tell you much about the destination; it tells you that you are on the right road.

As The Hollies told us, 'The road is long, with many a-winding turn', but knowing you are on the right road has a significant impact on decision making. Something which takes a business away from its chosen path can be attractive to that business in the short term. Perhaps it generates good revenue, or serves a customer well, and it can feel in the moment that it is worth taking the opportunity. A focus-on-forever check may reveal that it is a diversion not worth taking. A focus on forever can give us the courage to take the decisions that have to be taken to stay true to our intentions. On that long road, the focus is key to creating the success that you want.

Your endurance is your business's strength.

Forever is a long time

Thinking very long term is hard to do in the detail, but much easier to describe as an aspiration. The detail will come as you do the work, so think about the detail only insofar as it is able to get you moving, to start.

In the next section of this book I will describe a series of key strategic imperatives for any business seeking to be building better, and for any business leader seeking mastery. The strategies rely on having the knowledge to do, and the skills to perform, your best work. They provide a framework for you to gather experience and harness your growing expertise. It is from that foundation that insights will start to inform you, as your mastery develops.

A focus on forever allows us to see where our intentions are taking us. As we travel, we can make decisions against that aim: 'Does this help me achieve…?' That clarity also guides us to know where to focus for best effect today. To check our progress, we need to know ourselves (Chapter 5) and our skills (Chapter 6), and to be sure that we stay moving in the right direction we need to understand which signposts keep us on the right road (Chapter 9).

Forever is a long time, and focusing only on that distant aspiration might leave us exposed to the slings and arrows of outrageous (mis)fortune today. That is where strategy comes in: a focus on forever when you think strategically ensures that the day-to-day tactics you employ to deliver the strategy will be aligned. That is why, in Section 2, we will focus on five fundamental strategies that every successful business builds upon.

Reflect, review and redefine

Building better business is all about starting where you are. Whether the 'wall', those parts of the business that you are focused on, is long established and in need of repair or needs to be created from scratch, you have an opportunity. That opportunity is to rebuild it in the design you choose, to be deliberate and to design it on purpose.

Ways to focus on forever

1. Reflect on the work you are doing now and decide which elements are most in need of repair, replacement or reinforcement, making a list as you go.

2. Refine your list until it contains only the most critical elements that move you toward your long-term aspirations. Identify what that means you need to learn and where there will be opportunities to gain experience.

3. Redefine the processes and ways of working so that you will be more effective next time, and make time to record the data you need to evaluate your efforts effectively. Then start.

Section 2

Masterful Strategies

Working with many successful businesses and observing others over the years, I have identified five key areas of strategy. These areas are always well executed in successful businesses. Can you be successful without addressing them all? Perhaps, but you may not be performing at your best. Can you fail if you address them all effectively for your clients? Again, perhaps, yet I've never seen it happen. As I've worked with businesses addressing and improving strategy in each of these areas the businesses have got better – closer to the aspirations and ambitions of their owners.

After an overview of strategy in Chapter 4 (page 67) we'll discuss five key strategic areas:

1. Self – you, the business leader. See Chapter 5 (page 77).

2. Skills – what you do and how you deliver it. See Chapter 6 (page 111).

3. Systems – how your business operates and automates. See Chapter 7 (page 127).

4. Sales – how well it attracts new customers and how well they match the organisation's aims. See Chapter 8 (page 139).

5. Signposting – how well you tell others just what they need to know at the right time for them. See Chapter 9 (page 149).

4 Some Thoughts on Strategy

The essence of strategy is choosing what not to do.

– Michael Porter

Every business has one

There is a reality that every business has a strategy. There is another: not every business knows what that strategy is. Most dangerously though, there are businesses that have a stated strategy that simply doesn't match the actions that they take.

Strategy is one of those words that means different things to different people, so as a large part of this book discusses five key strategies for your business, I thought there should be clarity on the context in which the word is used here.

In one dictionary, strategy is defined as 'a detailed plan for achieving success in situations such as war, politics, business, industry, or sport, or the skill of planning for such situations', or 'a way of doing something or dealing with something'.[12] It is more in this second definition that I tend to place the meaning of strategy. In businesses, particularly small ones, the decisions

---

12 'Strategy'. Available at https://dictionary.cambridge.org/dictionary/english/strategy, accessed 30/08/2021.

on the ways of working are often driven by a relatively small number of people, perhaps just one – you. If strategy is defined, then, as a way of doing things, and if it is me doing them for my business, then my strategy is the result of my behaviours, thoughts, words and deeds.

Whatever I may think about the strategy I'm pursuing, I'm only really pursuing it if my behaviours are consistent with it. I'm sure you've experienced a business that makes clear statements about what it is intending from a strategic viewpoint, e.g. 'to be the world's best…' or similar, and yet its words and deeds, and the behaviour of its representatives, pull in a different direction. What does that do to your trust in that organisation?

Imagine that you are looking back from the end of the year. Imagine that you are saying to yourself, 'This was my finest year.' Imagine how that feels, and what those around you are saying about you. Imagine for a moment that all that you had done, said and thought had aligned to make that true.

Imagine who you will have become.

Then ask, 'Who am I now, and what do I need to do to become the person I imagine?' You'll think about how you are turning up in the world, what will make other people say those things about you, and what they say now. How will your behaviours have changed? What actions will you take? What knowledge will you have? What skills will you have honed? What words will you choose?

Write that down, be detailed, be explicit, be honest. Write down what is not yet true and what you will do to make it true. When you find the words that resonate, that make your heart beat faster and your soul soar, highlight them and refer to them often. Those words encapsulate your strategy.

Then, as Patrick Stewart would have said in *Star Trek* – 'Make it so, Number One.'

The nature of the beast

But what is strategy, really? Is it just a word to throw out to imply that some thinking has taken place? For some, that certainly is how they use it, but they shouldn't. Strategy is a little bit nebulous, so let's start by talking about what it is not. It's not how you do what you do – those are the tactics you employ to deliver a strategy. Nor is it just the vision, the mission or the culture: those describe your direction, approach, behaviours and environment. In many ways, strategy is how all of these work in harmony. Strategy will set direction, inform approach and define the ways of working to deliver it.

Some define strategy as the plan. My concern with this is that it leads many businesses to think that if they plan their activity then they have a strategy. Mostly they don't, they just have a to-do list, and that's not the same.

So, let's step back and ask what makes a great strategy. Maybe that can give us some clarity of what such a thing might be. Robert Rumelt, in his book *Good Strategy, Bad Strategy*, clarifies the difference between the good and the bad.[13] His thesis is that there are three elements to a great strategy: a clear diagnosis of the issue, a clear guiding policy and, only then, coherent actions.

A few years ago I was asked to put a project team together. Of course there was enormous pressure to get moving quickly, so I did, at least in terms of recruitment. The project had the full support of the senior management team (you would never take on leading a project that didn't have that, would you?), so resources weren't an issue. I sought out the best people

---

13 Rumelt, R. (2012). *Good Strategy Bad Strategy: The Difference and Why It Matters.* Profile Books Ltd.

and pulled the team together quickly. Nobody knew why they had been selected; a few wondered what they had done to deserve selection, and not in a good way. You can easily tell a team that doesn't have cohesion. Cliques between those who already know each other form. Whispers start and rumours are spread around the proverbial water cooler. It's not because anyone is subversive by nature; it's simply that we are at the start of a journey to collaboration, not its end. Trust is weak, uncertainty strong.

I've seen many projects where the leaders 'power through' by ignoring these signs, hoping that 'they will work it out' – 'they' can't, only 'we' can, as both the project team and project leaders have to be on the same page. I've a strategy for this situation, and it's worked consistently time and time again. We go for a walk.

Let me unpack that a little for you. The diagnosis is simple enough: trust is low, understanding weak, clarity of purpose misaligned. Each of those issues is best resolved by communication. My clear guiding policy is that trust matters most, and the most trust comes from deep collaboration. We would not do any work until the person being asked to do the work knew why it needed to be done, and more importantly why they were the best-placed person to do it.

It was too early in the collaboration (which we will look at in more detail in Chapter 6) for us to focus on those things, so we spent a week or two going for walks, in pairs and small groups, or as a whole team. I'd gently guide the discussions with ideas of what to share, all designed to build understanding of one another. Personal as well as business, talk about kids, and schools, and holidays and hobbies, talk about the project, find out what others know, and so on.

My bosses started to worry. Two weeks in and we were no nearer to understanding when tasks could be done. (My answer to that question was always 'sooner than we first thought possible – I'll be able to tell you exactly soon.') The team learned about each other, they formed friendships, they started sharing news and supporting each other in small personal matters, travelling together, making allowance for the parent of a disabled child to take a short-notice hospital appointment, and so on. When we turned to the planning of the project, people knew who had which skills, they knew where to get advice, they could support and help each other. There was collective understanding and responsibility. Many of the challenges of the interdependency of the workload were identified and then resolved as people walked. For me, there was no need to coordinate their day-to-day work; it was very liberating. I was able to deal with the external issues, negotiate for what was needed and the budget to get it, and so on.

About a month after we first pulled the team together, we issued the first plan. It was coherent, had reasonable contingency and reflected the depth of team understanding we had built. It was also wrong. A plan is never 'right' – and it is not the strategy. The team knew where they were heading and, when it changed, they adapted with the strategic goal in mind. In the end we delivered early, under budget.

The strategy is to build enduring trust, deepen understanding and clarify collective purpose because when you have all three the team will outperform even their own assessments. Starting out by going for walks together accelerates that.

Possibly the single best strategy for any business: slow down

Gandhi famously said, 'There's more to life than increasing its speed.' This applies to business as much as it applies to life.

Strategy is about delivering the long-term mission; it's a marathon, not a sprint, and that's why pacing is important. Everyday pressures force quick decisions to meet customers' needs, and there's no doubt that the world has accelerated. Operational speed means cutting corners and seeking a 'faster to market' edge over the competition that can hide the best long-term journey.

When geese are migrating, the bird who has to fly at the front breaks the air for those that follow. That takes extra energy and effort. The flock will naturally rotate the lead bird to share the load, and the flock goes further and faster as a result. There's a coherence in a flock of birds, an understanding, a system. That's strategic pace. Successful strategically paced companies will have the same coherence and understanding throughout the team.

Companies that focus on strategic pace find out how to deliver the same value in less time. They slow down enough to ensure that progress is continued along the appropriate track. One example of how this might be done is by taking the time to analyse and refine how they describe and communicate the real value of their product or service to their ideal customers. They ensure they are meeting the real needs of customers and validate authentic alignment to actual experience. Then they can communicate it much more effectively to others who may see those outcomes and sales accelerate as a result.

Companies who focus excessively on operational speed often don't pause to determine what's actually needed, instead following their established processes. They work hard, yet get a mediocre reaction. Ultimately, just wanting everything to be done at an ever-increasing pace kills innovation, removes insight and demotivates. It's unsustainable. There's very little learning, as there is no time, and so very little improvement.

Having strategically paced goals facilitates companies developing the appropriate tools and skills to truly meet their needs. They should focus on three areas:

- deep listening

- open learning

- effective re-skilling.

Strategically paced companies understand that alignment and clarity are essential for success, so they strive to get everyone on the same page. When there is alignment there are still mistakes, but there is no blame. Strategically paced businesses worry about, and work on, creating trusted and trusting environments. They know that the time needed to build trust, clarity and understanding is crucial, and together there is a confidence and assurance of what's to come that's both palpable and motivating. When there is a deep trust between client and supplier the relationship will be more enduring and that too helps you to be building better business.

When Holiday Inn found itself steadily losing market share in the 1980s and 90s, they developed superior customer service. They didn't seek to change their ethos in a moment, but took the strategically paced approach of spreading the need for change through compelling research, great communication inside the company, and being crystal clear about why the changes were necessary and in everyone's (staff, suppliers and customers) interest. Understanding your core values properly, communicating them well to others and using them as the filter for everything you do is at the heart of strategy. Understanding when to take action and pacing your work well makes its implementation far more powerful.

Companies implementing an effective strategic plan are always aware of the significance of solid leadership. This leadership should involve clear, open communication with the team. They must also be willing to listen to innovative ideas about how to improve. The leadership should be concerned with the end goal of the organisation and how the goals and the processes line up with company values.

Yet curiously, in the smallest businesses where the leadership and the delivery resource come together, sometimes in one person, there is often less alignment. I suspect that this is often because the leader doesn't feel the same need to think about how to communicate the strategy to themselves. Opportunities for valuable insights from others are lost as a result. That's why I recommend writing the goals down and talking them through with others even if ultimately you have to do the work yourself. The clarity that flows from such an analysis will make it far more robust.

General Motors' former director of planning and strategic initiatives, Nick Pudar, said that whenever he began to consider a new initiative, he started by meeting with all of those who would be involved and discussing with them their goals, their planned actions and the contributions they would need from other teams. By including those who were involved with the project in the initial conversation, Pudar and General Motors vastly improved the alignment within the organisation.

It's not just about time or stress: the Economist Intelligence Unit even found that companies who slowed down averaged

40 per cent more sales and 52 per cent more profits than companies who had made getting faster and faster their central priority.

In the project I discussed earlier, we delivered nearly a year ahead of the original target. The project team stayed together and delivered much more that enhanced and expanded the original project brief because, by slowing down at the start and building those strong relationships, everything was smoother afterwards. There was no waste, and many opportunities to go further emerged, yet it felt as if we were measured and reasonably paced throughout the whole project.

Slowly, slowly

Slowing down allows you to go further, faster. If you are the leader of your business and your team is small, then you will need to find the ways to make sure that you do take a moment now and again to slow down and lead your business from a strategic foundation.

Ways to slow down

1. Take a walk with a trusted business colleague (a member of your team, or an advisor, mentor or coach) and talk through the business topics that need your attention. Consider specifically how they align to your long-term ambitions.

2. Identify what you love about the way things will be, the way they are and the way they must change. Consider what skills you need and honestly assess if you have access to them already.

3. Write down your proposal in detail, and then read it critically a couple of days later. Reading it out loud (as if it was a staff briefing) is a powerful way to hear your own intentions.

5 Self

There is only one corner of the universe you can be certain of improving, and that's your own self.

– Aldous Huxley

So let's dive in and start looking at the first, and in some ways the most important, strategy. For some time, a business audit has been available at https://audit.williambuist.com. Many business owners and leaders have completed it, and in nearly all cases the answers suggest that businesspeople are relatively optimistic about themselves, and pessimistic about things they don't control (for example, sales volume). When I interview some who have completed it, it becomes obvious that for many there is a big dose of optimism about our own health and wellbeing. Perhaps that's people who are trying to convince themselves all is well, or it's a blind spot. Of course, not everybody is optimistic; a smaller number of people are deeply pessimistic about themselves. My conversations suggest that 'optimism' and' pessimism' aren't really the right labels here, as what I am describing is more about whether people externalise or internalise the challenges they know, deep down, that they face with themselves. Knowing that the words aren't quite the right descriptors hasn't helped me find better ones, but you can substitute them with ones that resonate for you, in your own assessment. On my (admittedly qualitative and subjective) analysis of the self-assessments, very few are realistic.

In reality, when we are considering the strategy for our own ability to do the work we love, neither excessive optimism nor pessimism is helpful, nor supportive of your long-term aspirations. Yet the audit reveals that it is hard to be accurate about assessing ourselves.

That's why this is the most important strategy for you to work on first.

It starts with you

Every small business is operated by a few people, sometimes only one. You. Even in the largest businesses there are always just a few people who have effective responsibility for the whole business.

In business, where you are one of the people, perhaps the only person, whose personal wellbeing is intimately linked to the wellbeing of the business, then one strategy you must have is to look after yourself. For me, that clear diagnosis meant that I formed a guiding principle to be emotionally aware, mentally resilient and physically well. Determining the coherent actions that I needed took quite some time – both to identify and then to deliver. That is, of course, another aspect of strategy. It has a long-term timescale.

I also gave some thought to seeking to understand *what* I needed to do, *how* to do it and *why* it was important.

Stephen Covey's excellent book, *Seven Habits of Highly Effective People*, opines that habits appear in the overlap of knowing what to do, how to do it and purpose, or why to do it at all. This is where excellent performance sits. When I thought about this model, my curiosity drove me to consider the other overlaps, where two of these, but not all three, were present. From that curiosity, I spent time considering and testing my thinking from practical observation of businesses and the people within them. If Covey was right and habits need all three to be present, what happens when someone knows what to do, knows why it's important, but doesn't know how to do it?

It's noticeable that it is unusual in business to be *habitually* truly effective. Most businesses often have two of these three elements dominant, most of the time. Knowing where you and your business are allows you to consider the best way to improve the effectiveness of your business.

In the business audit at https://audit.williambuist.com, I ask respondents to pick one word from three that they feel most strongly resonates with their own view of themselves. The three words are 'driven', 'energetic' and 'accomplished'. From the many responses, this diagnostic reveals the likelihood of (and what is lacking in) habit formation.

'Driven' implies that you most often know what the right thing to do is, and you know why it is important to do it. What's missing is detail on how to do that thing well. You tend to do the right work, but not well enough to get the results you expect or need as often as you would like.

'Energetic' implies that you most often know how to do the work you are doing and know why it is important. What's missing is the certainty to decide which of the things you could do is the best right now. As a result, you can do the wrong thing, and even though you do it well, it will not get the results you expect or need as often as you would like.

'Accomplished' implies that you most often know how to do the work and you know what to do, but are less sure about why the work matters. You may feel that you aren't getting the results you need, and customers may feel that you aren't as committed to their success as they would like. You probably sense this even if they aren't saying it to you directly.

The audit has shown a noticeable gender difference in the self-identified choice of the most resonating word. Women tend more often to choose accomplished or driven, while considerably more men than women choose energetic. We could spend a lot of time here reflecting on the causes and consequences of that difference, but much of that would be speculation on an interesting but ultimately unscientific study with a relatively small sample. It is, however, also reflected qualitatively in the discussions I have had with respondents.

What is clear in those discussions is how the differences play on the minds of the respondents. That led me to really understand how our emotional awareness plays a part in the decisions we take about what work to do next. When we make those decisions, it also becomes clear how much our mental resilience plays a part in how much attention we give to, and how well we perform, that work. Of course, our physical wellbeing affects both mental resilience and emotional awareness for everyone.

It seemed essential to me, in my business, to make sure that I was at my very best. Strategically that makes sense for every business owner or leader.

Let's explore those three aspects of the strategy for self in some more detail.

Emotional awareness

Until you make the unconscious conscious, it will direct your life and you will call it fate.

– C.G. Jung

Emotion and cognition

I've been aware for some years now of how my emotional state affects my cognition, my ability to learn from what was happening, to think logically and use my thinking processes to reason through challenges. I was not always so aware, and recognising that prompted me to research the topic.

Some psychological analyses of emotions studied them in isolation of their cognitive impact. For example, *The Nature of Emotion* is a book in which 24 of 'the most outstanding thinkers and writers on emotion' were asked to address twelve fundamental questions.[14] They did so almost in isolation of the impact on cognition. Interesting but, in my opinion, an unfortunate and limiting separation.

More recently, the link between emotions and logical reasoning has shown that there is 'a clear effect of emotions on reasoning performance'.[15] This work goes on to say, 'Participants in negative mood performed worse than participants in a positive mood, but both groups were outperformed by the neutral mood reasoners'. I found that a fascinating insight.

14 Ekman, D., Ekman, P. and Davidson, R. (1994). *The Nature of Emotion: Fundamental Questions.* Oxford University Press.
15 Jung, N., Wranke, C., Hamburger, K. and Knauff, M. 'How Emotions Affect Logical Reasoning: Evidence from Experiments with Mood-Manipulated Participants, Spider Phobics, and People with Exam Anxiety'. *Frontiers in Psychology* 5 (10 June 2014). https://doi.org/10.3389/fpsyg.2014.00570

This final point is key, I think. It highlights why, on those days when I wake up feeling down, my ability to deliver would also clearly, and not unexpectedly, suffer. Yet, it also explains why, on days when I felt very positive, my ability to deliver was also diminished. I could slip into a negative spiral of heightened emotional states leading to poor delivery that would leave me feeling emotionally depressed. Now I am conscious of that risk when I am in a very positive or negative mood. When I am, I tend to change the work I do, or even take a break from it, so that I can return in a frame of mind more attuned to my best performance.

Conscious awareness of our true emotional state can be hard if our minds have been trained over years to suppress or relegate emotional awareness to our subconscious. Being able to recognise and take action to change our emotional state, especially when it is at a positive or negative extreme, is a skill worth honing.

In order to highlight how I came to be more aware of the impact on my own business endeavours, I spent some time reflecting on the impact of emotions following the death of my mother in 2011. I'm not suggesting that you need to lose a parent or a loved one (and suffer the associated grief) to get to the understanding I now have – that was just how it happened to come to me. It's now more than ten years ago and, of course, I still miss mum, and all her foibles, every day. However, the impact of that time for me has been profound. It was her gift to me although I did not know it at the time.

To give you context, I need to provide you with a little bit of background.

Unlocking subconscious emotions

During the Second World War, my mother worked in the War Office at Number 1, Whitehall Place, London. She married my father in a small ceremony in Caxton Hall, Westminster in 1944. He was based in Manchester in a reserved occupation with ICI, improving polyurethane foams that were being developed to insulate Lancaster bombers. After the war, my mother rejoined him in Manchester, her job having come to an end, as the roles were reallocated to returning soldiers. These were very different times.

She, like anyone who had worked closely with others, had formed strong relationships with her workmates. They kept in touch in a variety of ways, but ultimately they formed a correspondence magazine. This was a round robin collection of letters from each participant, sent in a folder. As it arrived, you would take your letter out of the folder. It was annotated with comments and questions, and you would write the next entry to inform and develop the conversation. It was a blog before the internet – a private social network before the idea of modern computing had even begun.

It required care: the information was personal, these were people who knew each other well and were sharing sometimes intimate details of family and friends, so confidentiality was important. They chose to use pen names. My mother chose Abelard.

Peter Abelard was born in 1079 in France.[16] He became a philosopher and studied the nature of thought itself, and ultimately it was in ethics that Abelard showed the greatest activity of philosophical thought. He examined the ideas of

---

16 'Peter Abelard'. Available at: https://en.wikipedia.org/wiki/Peter_Abelard, accessed 23/01/2021.

the importance of subjective intention as a key determinant of the moral value of human action. Nearly a millennium later his writing on those topics still has the attention of philosophical thinking. However, it was his love for Héloïse d'Argenteuil that become legendary.[17] In Héloïse's writing, many ideas of feminism were formed. She and Abelard exchanged letters on questions of spirituality, scripture, love and hurt.

Because they were writers of letters, and because my mother's name was Eloise, my mother chose the pen name Abelard – Ab for short. Her letters, and the commentary, have all been kept. All my childhood (and my sisters') was recorded in monthly detail, my father's progress and slip-ups, my mother's fears, the years looking after her mother, losing friends, all the events of the world commented on for over 50 years.

In the mid-1970s my father left ICI and set up his own consultancy business through which he worked as a director of a local rubber chemicals firm, as the editor of trade magazines and leading the trade bodies in his chosen industry. He called that consultancy business Abelard Management Services, and it ran until he retired in the early 1990s. My father died in 1999, after a slow decline from chronic obstructive pulmonary disease (COPD). In 2004, when I started my business, the domains (not a concern my father ever had) and the company name were still available, and Abelard was reborn. I know that choice made my mother smile.

In May 2007, my mother, who had been exhibiting symptoms of atrial fibrillation for some time, had a serious stroke. She lost the use of her left leg and arm, and for a while her speech was affected. Her days of independent living were over, and for

---

17 'Héloïse'. Available at: https://en.wikipedia.org/wiki/Héloïse, accessed 23/01/2021.

another four years she lived a comfortable, if unimaginative and uninspiring life in a nursing home. During that time I visited at weekends when it was possible. Her mind was often absent, and her ability to concentrate was almost entirely lost. Yet in moments of lucidity we still would do many normal things. We'd laugh about the politicians – well, there was little else to do; if one took them seriously, we would have cried or raged. Sometimes we would talk about the family, the things that had happened over the years, or discuss the weather. She couldn't hold a newspaper easily so I'd sometimes read to her. On occasion we would struggle with a crossword, and sometimes exchange a cross word too. It was a little bit of normality for her in a place where normality had no real meaning.

In 2011 it became clear she had reached a decision. Her appetite dwindled, or she chose not to eat much and refused to be fed by other means. There was an inevitable outcome, and on 4 December 2011 she passed away peacefully.

A few weeks, maybe two or three months later, I woke up with a start. 'Abelard, It's mine now!' I thought. Yet as I reflected on that thought, I felt something of a cold sweat. A realisation that for all those years since 2004 it had not, emotionally, been mine. I'd run the business for her, for the memory of my father, but not really for me.

Of course it had always actually been my business, but emotionally there was another owner – a prior consideration that meant I had an emotional roadblock to developing the business my way. The emotional block meant decisions were coloured by and judged against an internal questioning I had from an invisible board asking me to justify everything, with no means of getting any affirmation. That was a stress-inducing and ultimately fruitless situation from which no one can escape unscathed.

So, I pondered, what else was there, of which I have no knowledge, that challenges me to be something I am not, and stops me from being who I truly am? There was a lot. Far too much. I had too often questioned the purpose of the very things that would have helped me to achieve my goals. Too often taken a path to a different ambition.

It was time for some hard thinking.

Give it a name

For a long time afterwards I thought that this was something unique, just about my situation, my personal circumstances, and superficially that is, of course, true. Some time later I raised the issue at a mastermind group that I belonged to. To my initial surprise, people related to the situation and had shared those feelings. Everyone had felt the same sense of challenge that these emotional blocks create.

Since then I have discussed the impact of emotional blocks with businesspeople in all walks of life. For those who recognised the challenge, all had experienced, at some point, a release when an emotional block was identified, faced and unlocked. Indeed I sometimes wonder if the only thing that really holds us back is our emotional state. Whether that is fear, trepidation, uncertainty, frustration, anger, or whatever emotion we are feeling at a particular moment in the course of our daily work. Not the same one every day, of course, or even every minute, but present nonetheless.

That realisation led me to seek out techniques to help me to be more aware of what is happening with my own emotions, and then, gradually, to be better able to deal with them. The simplest of these techniques is called 'affect labelling'; this is the action of describing the emotions you are feeling with words. It has an immediate impact on the emotional state, swiftly reducing negative feelings caused by the emotions.

A study by Shinpei Yoshimura and Tomoko Morimoto identified a mechanism which showed that the processing of language in the brain interrupted the way that the emotion interacts with the amygdala.[18] (The amygdala is a part of the brain that is thought to be associated with emotional memory; in relation to strong negative emotions like fear or anger, it is believed that it can drive current expressed behaviour because of the historically associated memories). By naming the current emotion there's a pattern interrupt which seems, according to the study, to have a significant impact. Using imaging techniques the study showed that affect labelling produced increased activity in a single brain region, the right ventrolateral prefrontal cortex. Further they saw that activity in the right ventrolateral prefrontal cortex is inversely proportional to activity in the amygdala.

It took me a while to make identifying and labelling emotions a habit. Journaling helped me to do that. When I knew my emotions were a little 'out of whack', writing them down helped. Reading what I had written had more impact; reading what I had written out loud had even more. I learned that if something triggered a disappointment, that could quickly, unless I interrupted it with these techniques, become frustration. I've learned that frustration makes me flit from task to task. A failure to resolve the frustration can lead to anger. A chain of emotions that first triggered behaviour (flitting from task to task) that then triggered other emotions, anger at failing to focus being the obvious outcome here.

---

18 Shinpei, Y. and Morimoto, T. 'Affect Labeling Disrupts Amygdala Activity in Response to Affective Stimuli'. *The Proceedings of the Annual Convention of the Japanese Psychological Association* 82, no. 0 (25 September 2018): 2EV-073-2EV – 073. https://doi.org/10.4992/pacjpa.82.0_2EV-073

My challenge was that I could sometimes only notice the emotional states when they were already a long way down a chain like that, perhaps only at its end, when the anger has taken over behaviour. I don't want to imply I was angry all the time – it was rare, but when it arrived it was hard to get back to an even keel. I learned that when I did identify an emotional state, it was also useful to reflect on the chain of events and feelings that had triggered it. Labelling the anger would diminish it. I nurtured the habit of being curious about causation. Why was I just angry? That helped me to identify the causative trigger, flitting from task to task in the example above. Next time I noticed myself flitting I could ask what emotional state I was in and recognise the frustration. Curiosity about that leads to identifying the disappointment.

Over time, understanding the chains as they affect me has meant that I have taken more intentional control, which is one of the most profound capabilities that this attention has delivered.

My 'morning pages' is my journal of thoughts and reflections and I often included my thoughts about the emotions and feelings I had recently experienced. Being able to see those in conjunction with the activities and coincident thoughts did, over time, throw up some patterns for me that were useful in understanding what affected me. Affect labelling has become a habit that has given me a sense of calm and confidence that I wish I had had years ago. I recommend practising it, getting proficient at it, and making it a habit. It becomes part of your own self-mastery, and in the wider scheme of things I don't believe that you can master a topic until you have mastered your emotional connection to it.

In fact journaling can go deeper than that. Studies by Gortner, Rude and Pennebaker show that expressive writing, even for only a few days (they tested this by asking students to write on just three consecutive days) can have an immediate effect on the symptoms of negativity and depression.[19] Their work reinforces my experience, that journaling allows us to see who we really are, and therefore how we might change if we choose to do so. Perhaps not even 'if' we choose to do so; somehow, for me at least, that writing allows the better person to step onto the page, and when I then read my own words, to step back into me. That may all sound a little new age, and perhaps it is, but it works for me and it might for you too.

Emotional leverage

You will recall that I mentioned earlier that our performance when we have negative emotions is not as good as when we have a positive one, but it is best when our emotions are neutral.

That's given me permission to think about how to use negative energy rather than to fight it. Over the years I've found that on those days where I know I am feeling down, to see if I can focus on work that brings me joy, done carefully, that can help improve my mood and up my productivity. Perhaps a similar technique could work for you.

There are some elements which I have identified that are important to my ability to lift a negative mood. First, my to-do list is not a place of joy, so I don't look at that. My mind is a wonderful receptacle of what is needing to be done anyway; it has imperfect recall, but it also doesn't remind me of the full extent of the workload; it just brings things to mind one at a time.

---

19 Gortner, E-M., Rude, S. S. and Pennebaker, J. W. 'Benefits of Expressive Writing in Lowering Rumination and Depressive Symptoms'. *Behavior Therapy* 37(3) 1 September 2006: 292–303. https://doi.org/10.1016/j.beth.2006.01.004

Second, the jobs that will bring me joy when they are finished are not the same as the jobs that bring me joy in the work itself. Sometimes simply focusing on an element that brings joy in the moment is what I need to do.

For example, I draw great joy in photography, joy in the process, joy from being a photographer. Grabbing the camera and taking a few shots of a flower in the garden can completely shift my mood. I use my photographs whenever I can in my writing, in articles, on websites and so on. I need new content all the time. Quite often those images, taken when I am seeking to lift my mood, capture the 'moodiness' of the moment; they tell a story. When they do I sense enjoyment, excitement and a positive lift. I have clients who walk, go riding, write or sing to make these same shifts. What is it in your life that you could do to achieve that?

What we are all doing is leveraging the power of joy to lift our mood in the moments when it needs support.

The impacts of your own emotional awareness on your business

As owners of small businesses, how we turn up each day depends on how well we are emotionally. That is bound to have a big impact on how the business will perform.

Business after business run by dedicated people determined to do their best has stumbled and underperformed because the owner's emotional state affected the business negatively. Often they focused so much on the business that they forgot to look after themselves and that made them emotionally challenged in a vicious cycle that leads to the wrong destination.

Do not let that happen to you.

Mastery of your emotional self

Earlier I highlighted that every business has a strategy although it may not know what it is. Even, perhaps especially, when a business doesn't know what its strategy is, the rest of us can see it. Collectively we see the behaviours and actions and words that ultimately define it. Is your strategy one of confusion, misdirection, uncertainty, or is it clear in everything you do? If it is clear to you, is it also clear to others?

When we think about the journey to mastery it's worth reflecting that when we are explorers and novices, when we don't know enough to know better, it's hard to have a strategy at all; it's probably impossible to have a good one. As practitioners, it's having a good strategic foundation that frees you to work on building expertise. Understanding why particular strategies deliver value and how their implementation will change who we are is one of the skills of the master.

Yet when it comes to ourselves, unless we are self-observant and self-aware and able to both spot and use our emotions in the service of our strategies, then they will always have an opportunity to trip us up.

Writing in my journal every day, being transparent (to myself) about my state of mind, and reflecting on what has worked (and what could be improved) has become a daily ritual. At the start of every day it is sometimes little more than a ramble of nonsense, but on some days it brings a clarity that is insightful. The nonsense is an important part; it's the way we think. I'd struggled to make journaling a habit, given the self-imposed desire not to write nonsense. It became a habit when I let that go. I realised that it is the *act* of journaling that matters, not the *content* of the journal. Much is never read again; it's purpose was to be written, not to be read.

You may also get a lot of benefit from identifying what it is that brings you joy (and the context in which that joy is strongest).

Mental resilience

*Joy, collected over time, fuels resilience –
ensuring we'll have reservoirs of emotional
strength when hard things do happen.*

– Brené Brown[20]

Take your umbrella

Resilience is a word that has become, in my opinion, rather devalued in recent times. Too often talk of resilience is used to describe little more than managing to think clearly. For me, resilience is something much more fundamental.

Resilience is defined by dictionary.com as 'the power or ability of a material to return to its original form, position, etc. after being bent, compressed, or stretched. The ability of a person to adjust to or recover readily from illness, adversity, major life changes. The ability of a system or organisation to respond to or recover readily from a crisis, disruptive process.'[21]

Mental resilience, then, is the capability of our minds to return to their original state when we are put under mental pressure. The definition implies that, when things bend our minds out of shape or compress or stretch the mind, resilience means reverting to its unstressed mode. That last point is important, because when our minds are stretched, perhaps with new

---

20 Brown, B. (2013) 'The Fast Track To Genuine Joy'. Available at www.huffpost.com/
entry/finding-happiness-brene-brown_n_4312653, accessed 23/05/2022.
21 'Resiliency'. Available at: www.dictionary.com/browse/resiliency, accessed
18/11/2021.

skills or knowledge, we do not want resilience. The new state should be maintained.

It's my intention to define mental resilience as something that allows us to recover from forces that put the mind into a place where it is performing less well than it did. Perhaps that means logical thinking, and critical thinking, are diminished, or decision making is poorer. Perhaps it's where the troubled mind interferes with sleep or relationships or the ability to perform normal activities.

Is this the same as mental toughness? No, I don't think it is. Toughness is a more proactive approach to avoiding situations that could give rise to negative pressures in the first place. It's that defensive mechanism that those who advocate for it use to avoid being knocked down at all. While that might make it less likely that someone is affected by the challenges they face, there will still be a time when they do fall, and having the skills for mental resilience, and a strategy to employ those skills, will reward them. We need a level of toughness to choose to do some of the more difficult things, but we need resilience for when they don't work out.

Resilience comes from the preparatory work. It's a bit like taking an umbrella with you on a sunny morning when you will be out all day. It means you will be ready, should it rain. It also acknowledges that there will be rainy days sometimes. Toughness focuses on ignoring the rain if it falls; resilience puts the umbrella up.

The 2008 banking crisis

My business was about four years old and I was working on several projects with large clients when the news broke that Northern Rock had queues of people outside seeking to withdraw their money. The bank had used financial instruments in its commercial operations that would prove to be worthless (or close to it) and the word had got out that the bank was in difficulty. Our modern banks, quite legitimately, are heavily leveraged, meaning they don't hold our cash – it's being used to fund other activities. If everyone turns up at once to withdraw their money, the bank will quickly run out of cash.

At the time I thought it was a local problem, but quickly we started to recognise that reorganisation and bundling of American sub-prime loans into financial instruments and derivatives was little more than gambling. They were failing to provide the returns or even the value that they had been purchased for. As their value collapsed so the balance sheets of the organisations holding these instruments began to turn negative, which spiralled the impact out of control. The nature of globalisation now meant everywhere was impacted, as banks traded debt and other financial instruments on global markets. Sub-prime American mortgage debt was affecting a UK regional bank's ability to meet the withdrawal requirements of its customers.

Within three weeks, all my client work had stopped. That's a challenge, and it's one that I ignored, or at least dismissed as a short-term issue. 'It will be tough, but I am tough' was my logic. I was, of course, completely wrong, and it was a mistake that nearly cost me the business. The real mistake – apart from not recognising the impact mortgage debt in America would have on the revenue for a small British consultancy business – was thinking that waiting it out was being resilient. Rather, it was being stupid. That's perhaps harsh; hindsight tells me that it was the lack of similar experience that was the issue. Lack of experience, not just of that situation but of anything similar.

That taught me to assess each situation by asking some questions and following through on the logic that the thinking initiates. Those questions, by the way, are: 'What do I know?', 'What do I really know?' and 'What can I compare this to?' At the time, though, I didn't ask those questions. It wasn't my ignorance of the situation that made me stupid, it was my failure to be curious.

As the situation continued and my bank balance started to fall, I made poorer and poorer decisions. My mind was anxious, then scared, my sleep disrupted, my relationships strained – all of which piled more pressure on and bent my mind further out of shape. This wasn't something that happened over a few days or even weeks. It was gradual and made up of many small changes, which had an additive effect. A challenge here, a bill there, a credit card account that no longer could be paid off and then the spiral as the debt mounted month after month. A lack of client work, which feeds my soul from the joy it brings, but its absence sapped my strength and left me enervated and lethargic. Ultimately, I was giving up, becoming isolated in my own mind, where the lack of resilience meant every blow was felt viscerally. The dark days became black and the best days of that time were still darker than any of the days when I truly lived.

I'm not sure if this was depression; I never sought help (yet another poor decision) so nothing was ever diagnosed, but looking back now I know this was a bad place to be. For three years – three long years – the business was struggling. It turned out I had to wait until after my mother died in 2011 before I started examining the emotions I was feeling, and started learning about how to make myself more mentally resilient.

Those lessons were hard won, and too slowly. Far too slowly. It's worth noting how, in 2020, when the global pandemic struck, my actions were very different. Rather than 'wait it out' I took immediate action. The following year was very good as a result. Yet many of my friends' businesses suffered an immediate and catastrophic loss of earning power as lockdowns did their work on the virus. For some of them, I saw the same descent into depression and inaction that, for me, happened in 2008.

My business crime scene

Yet the lessons were learned. Pretty quickly, once they were learned, some things did start to change. I redefined, even redesigned, my business model to make it, and myself, more resilient, and I shifted my own attitude to how I reacted to stressors. A key lesson here is how attitude matters, how the way you turn up every day affects how well or badly that day affects the mind. I let go of the past – and not just metaphorically.

I want to be clear here; this was not some bright awakening that happened in a blinding flash of the obvious, but a very slow shift from darkness to shadows, to grey to a false dawn or several, to gradual change on gradual change. Months, not weeks. I've often worried about the way some people talk about mental health, mental resilience, depression and recovery – as if they were almost switches. This is not a psychology book – I'm not a psychologist and make no pretence to advise on mental health. I just want you to know that nobody is expecting you, from where you are, to change your mental resilience by saying that you will. You cannot flip a switch. All I can do is share my experience, with the intention that as you read about it you can take some elements to apply in your business, in your context, and see how they work out for you.

Letting go of the past meant understanding it. I had to spend time thinking about the chain of events, of my reactions to them, labelling the emotions and matching those to how I felt, and thinking about how the business performed (or didn't) at those times. It's not easy thinking, and it's very easy (especially if one is already feeling guilty at the poor results, frustrated by one's own performance and choices) to slip back into more despair. I did. Often. I kept asking, 'What is it about this that I am judging?', and 'How could I view it differently?'

Through that process, business choices started being examined with a fresh eye. Rather than the self-focused 'You let that sale slip through your fingers', I started to reframe the accusation as a question: 'How can I make the offer more compelling and authentic?' Gradually it did change; the answers to my questions were all about clarity, strategy and implementation.

Looking back, it's no surprise to me that the answer to the near death of my business was CSI. *CSI* is also the name of a long-running TV show about forensic science. *Crime Scene Investigations* examines the evidence, reconstructs what happened and reflects on it in order to truly understand the crime. In many ways my business, at this time, was a crime scene.

CSI is predominantly about understanding knowing where you are (clarity), knowing where you want to be (strategy) and the steps to get there (implementation) – CSI is a framework for making strategy work in the real world.

An aside: most businesses are hopelessly vague about what they do, for the perfectly valid reason that it has evolved and changed over time. Parts of the organisation are still working as they used to be. That's confusing for those outside. I also learned that most organisations don't see themselves as lacking sufficient clarity. That's mainly because they are clear in their own minds about what they do, but have insufficient clarity in how they communicate that to others.

Creating safe ground

How does all this map into your business?

First, the clarity that came from reflecting on the causes and impacts of the decisions I was taking provided me with some safe areas. When you know (for sure) that when you do something a particular way it will produce a particular result, that reliability provides certainty, a foundation. A place to return to when you are out of shape. Resilience.

Usually though, when we are building better business, we are looking to improve and change. Where did I want to get to? If the consequence of a change is positive then you can choose that route more often. In doing so you will create more safe ground, and that clarity makes it easier to be more resilient to the next challenge.

When I started this thinking and being more strategic about how to make improvements, I found I was trying to be too detailed, to describe everything, but as we'll uncover in Chapter 9 – signposts don't carry all the detail; they set direction. It was when I recognised the need to be visionary that I started to regain control of my mind's ability to plan.

Spurious accuracy, that detailed planning of all the steps on a journey that will look different as soon as the first step is taken, saps mental resilience. A vision, a couple of signposts to set the route, *that's* what's needed. A clear idea of where you are going to, and some thought on how you will know you are on course and then plan the near-term – three months roughly, a month with some care, a week in detail and today precisely.

These days I take a few minutes at the start of each day to map out that day, and an hour each Monday morning to plan the week, with the end in mind, with the vision. This book came about because I had a vision of it existing. I knew that it would require time, effort and energy to complete, and that regular writing as part of my routine would do that.

The CSI approach gave me the resilience to do the hard work of writing and editing and thinking and rewriting. Now you hold in your hands the product of that work.

Physical wellbeing

Your health matters

As a business owner there's a reality none of us can escape from: individual health and business health are linked. When one falters, the other likely will too. If your business has a challenge that puts a lot of stress on the owner, it's likely they will see health impacts, mental or physical, as a result of that stress. If the owner is unwell, the business loses leadership focus and there is a likelihood it will suffer too.

One striking example of that came from my good friend Bryony Thomas. Bryony is an expert marketer who had built a successful marketing and training organisation mostly from the force of her own determination. By her own admission she was inclined to take things on herself, to carry the burden of responsibility, and to work too long and too hard. She was diagnosed with pancreatic cancer and it seemed likely she had just a few weeks to live. Major operations, chemotherapy, the love of her family and the support of her friends saved her life. Fortunately for Bryony her business was resilient enough to survive that. Many, perhaps most, would not. That said, she had been considering some major structural changes to her business to continue its expansion, and those didn't go ahead. Instead, today, she is rebuilding the business to a different model – one that doesn't require her to do everything, one that is a team effort and one that is much more resilient. As Bryony has regained her strength, she and her family are thriving, and so is the business.

This link, I've learned over the years, and which Bryony's experience shows, is much more closely aligned than most give it credit for. One reason is that changes in a business take time to work through into the results. When an owner is distracted by health issues, customers don't leave immediately, but more leave earlier than they would otherwise. Fewer referrals are made, and a few months later the business is a long way from optimal. Equally, when a business owner deals with health issues and focuses on the business, it can take months, sometimes even a year or two, for that effort to pay dividends.

Throughout life, when cause and effect are separated in this way the separation can harm decision making. It's easier for any analysis if the underlying cause is coincident in time with the effect. When they are separated we can assign the cause of change to a more recent action that appears to be the trigger, so we need care to be sure we understand the links. We also need to recognise the time that some things take to be realised. Often, I see businesses giving up on activities that have not yielded a result, but which would if they kept up the focus. We call these allocation errors.

Let me tell a short story to illustrate this from my own experience.

I took a bite of the most wonderfully cooked food and chewed slowly, savouring how the chef had created such a wonderful melange of flavours. As I chewed, they developed and matured, giving a richness and depth to the experience.

I swallowed and then felt a tightness at the line of my ribcage – something wasn't right. Another swallow made me more uncomfortable. The food was stuck. I drank some water, and with a sharp pain I quickly returned to normal.

Those symptoms persisted, became more and more frequent, and after a trip to the doctors, and then the hospital, they decided to explore them, and the severe acid reflux that came with them. After a battery of tests I was diagnosed with a hiatus hernia – a weakness in the diaphragm where the oesophagus passes through. At times that was causing food to get stuck on the wrong side of the diaphragm. Not comfortable, but not life-threatening, and not recommended for an operation as the success rates are not great, and complications can be serious. I was prescribed omeprazole, a type of drug known as a proton pump inhibitor, to reduce the production of stomach acid and limit the impact of acid reflux. Heartburn was a daily discomfort at the time.

Now, I don't know about you, but I didn't much fancy taking long-term drugs for anything, and the doctor had prescribed these 'for the rest of your life'. I was already taking a steroid inhaler twice daily to ward off asthma and the risk of pneumonia.

I stopped and looked at myself in the mirror. Fat William looked back. I was overweight – not obese – perhaps a couple of stone too heavy. I was unfit too. I needed some big changes – I decided that I needed to treat this as a two-year project. I'd watch my diet, increase my exercise, and be more intentional about my health.

I realised, with that blinding flash of the obvious that leaves you slapping your forehead in a state of frustrated realisation, that my health had been slipping for a few years, and that these symptoms were an effect of taking my eyes off my own health needs.

As I've discussed, I'd become aware of my emotions and the impact they were having on me and I decided to use the same techniques. I also, at about the same time, bought technology that could monitor some aspects of this for me. My levels of exercise, for example. Over the course of a couple of years the weight came off. I took up swimming a couple of times a week and that helped too, and I was much more intentional about how I ate. Against some advice I measured my weight every day, but was conscious not to let emotional responses to occasional weight gain stop my longer-term intentions for casting it off. I never wanted it to be a sprint – that would always result in failure for me.

Keeping your business fit

There are so many corollaries with business that I am sure you can see them already. Most businesses carry too much weight in places, and as things change in the world they find their processes have unnecessary, flabby elements. Habits mean many of these, less than ideal, approaches just get repeated. When processes change they tend to be added to, not redesigned. Processes that were automated to great fanfare now happen because they always did, not because they are still needed.

Businesses also provide a form of process medicine; they layer new systems onto existing systems to correct what the earlier system did that now works against the business. If we fix physical health with a drug and get a side effect, we may need a second drug to treat the side effect, and then a third and so on. When a new infection appears, the doctors struggle to spot it, or to know if you need different drugs or if it's just another side effect.

Over time the layers of processes make it hard to find where the problem is, and harder to fix it. It's a kind of collective madness, but in the cauldron of the day-to-day, under great pressure of work, it's often easier, quicker and simpler to create a sticking plaster than to redesign. This is why software coders talk about patches, isn't it? Technology doesn't help: as each year passes more computing power is available. A process that used to take an hour for the computer to work through now takes a minute, or at least it could if the patches, fixes and opportunities to add to the code without fixing it didn't add to the need for more computational grunt. Still, it only takes 15 minutes now so that's better than before – right? Perhaps, but if with some redesign it could be done in a few seconds, that really would be a success. When patched code breaks, the hunt is on: where is the fault? Is it the original code? Is it the patch?

Every time a business adds a fix it also builds a potential constraint. Mastery is so often about simplifying – going back to the foundations and building afresh.

Building afresh

How can that be done? I think, somewhat like physical wellbeing, the first step is to identify the end state you seek. For me, that was about losing some weight and being more intentional about what I ate. In business, understanding where there is fat and what is lean in the business is important. What causes the fat to be there? One at a time, decide what needs to change and look at it from the inputs (the food) to the outputs. Work out the best way to deliver those outputs now without reference to 'the way it is done'. Then you can compare and start thinking about how to change from the current way to the better way.

In business we sometimes have to trade benefits and costs, and it is always worth remembering that perfect systems probably don't exist. There are compromises to make and we should make them intentionally, not by accident. That said, I do recommend doing something similar to the system of 'best before' and 'use by' dates on food, but for business processes and systems. A 'review by' date can help achieve some certainty that at least now and again you will review the process. We will talk more about how to approach systems, and review them, in Chapter 7.

Our best selves

When the weight came off me a few symptoms started to change. I stopped feeling that 'stuck food' discomfort when eating, and acid indigestion became a memory. I stopped taking the omeprazole. A hay fever season came and went without ever feeling like I needed help to breathe. Without the reminders from my body, I started to forget to take the steroid inhaler and gradually I stopped using it completely. At the time of penning these words I've remained asymptomatic for well over two years. I'm not saying that the hiatus hernia that was diagnosed has miraculously healed – it hasn't, but without the additional visceral fat I was carrying, the pressure on it has reduced to the point where it doesn't cause other symptoms. Is my lung function fully restored? No, but it is under less strain and so can cope with the day-to-day without needing a drugs boost.

The real thing to note, though, is not the symptoms or their absence; it is that I am living differently, living a different life from the one I had been living. My understanding of the way I worked meant I could work with genuine constraints and build on the real foundations of who I am. Some might call it alignment or authenticity – not me. I just call it 'sensible', working with what is there, in the way that works best, to get the best from it.

That is so easy to say, yet it took me six decades to work it out. Perhaps I'm slow, but it is more likely that there really is a need to have the wisdom first. To understand how emotions affect you, and the resilience to work through the hard times before one truly knows what does work best, and how to access it. Mastery and wisdom are collaborators, mutual supporters of our best selves.

I recognised how the level of exercise (and the quality of it) and what I ate and drank had an undoubted effect on my business performance too. I improved them all by eating more intentionally, exercising more regularly, managing my weight and my fitness.

If you want to be commended or criticised on your diet, shape, fitness and looks, there are plenty of others out there ready to voice an opinion. My point here is not to tell you what you need to do, but to give you an opportunity to reflect on what you want. Forget what the world wants you to be. What do you want to be? It's easy to let it just happen and then shrug and say you are what you are, but you can choose. It took illness to make me choose, but you can do that today without waiting.

The intricate dance

An aspect of the time I have spent looking inwards, labelling and acknowledging emotions and their impact on my resilience, and considering my physical wellbeing, was the realisation of how interlinked all these things were. What food I ate, how much alcohol, water, caffeine and fizzy drinks I consumed (and when) affected my sleep, my sleep affected my moods and emotions, my emotions drove my resilience and ability to cope with setbacks.

An unexpected external frustration could trigger comfort eating that would lead to a disturbed night. The tiredness would lead to more emotional responses and a tendency to reach for high-calorie foods to counter the exhaustion. In that exhaustion, I might forget to apply the skills I have to achieve the things I want. Thinking was clouded, as contextual connections between different experiences were lost. That leads to rework, error and more frustration. It is an intricate and complex dance that needs choreography, planning, thinking through, and a willingness to get it wrong and learn and try again.

I have days when the dance slips, when my emotions take a front seat when I would prefer them to be silent. I have days when I have to walk away from what I am doing because I feel out of balance. Meditation can soothe a racing mind and allow emotions to slip away. Exercise and the cadence of walking help me too. Identifying any imbalance, from the choreography of our emotional awareness, mental resilience and physical wellbeing, can be hard, but my goodness, it is worth it.

On other days the dance is joyful. My awareness of my emotions has an impact on my resilience, and I feel well, eat well, sleep soundly and wake refreshed. I welcome those days, and as I practised, meditated and got fitter, those days became more frequent. I could not have written this book if they were not normal for me now.

Building the choreography

When I eat intentionally, get enough exercise, sleep well, and a challenge rears its head, it is often quickly resolved, almost by itself. The intricate dance tends to be a cycle, virtuous if you have a hold of it, vicious if you let it go. The way in, the way to get a hold, that works for me is to be curious about your emotions, to find the moment, force it if needs be, to listen to the chemical soup of our bodies and the impact those chemicals have on our emotions and thoughts. I find that labelling the sensation, even saying it out loud ('I'm frustrated', 'I'm angry') allows me to be curious about the label. That makes it much easier to wrap it up and put it to one side.

The emotional awareness I achieved had a beneficial side effect too: a calmer, more confident outlook that I found made me more resilient. I was able to cope with the ups and downs of life with a more pragmatic mindset. As a consequence, I had more time to walk and to savour food and drink rather than rush them down before getting back to whatever was stressing me out at the time. Which meant it no longer stressed me. Comfort eating and snacking fell away and I lost some weight and got fitter. By affect labelling, I'd understood my emotions, built resilience and improved my physical wellbeing. Will that work for everyone?

I talked to my good friend, and client, George Anderson. George's specialism focused on how aspects of physical wellbeing affected our ability to perform well holistically. Both of us have experienced the links between emotional awareness, mental resilience and physical wellbeing, yet our focus has been on different starting points. George used his focus on the physical aspects and found that has given him greater mental resilience as a consequence. He too has a clear understanding of his emotional state. In many conversations exploring others' experiences, the same things are seen.

Clive Woodward, in his book *Winning*, speaks to the challenges of working under pressure, which we all have to do from time to time, and how good our decision making is.[22] He opines that it is the ability to 'Think Correctly Under Pressure' (T-CUP) that was one key point of difference between winning and losing the Rugby World Cup.

As a result of many conversations I suspect that, given the amygdala's role in associating strong, often negative, emotions with elements of memory that emotional awareness, mental resilience and physical wellbeing are linked in a coordinated way. Improving any one of them will often improve all three.

When we are in control of our emotions, when we are resilient to the external changes imposed on us, and when we are physically well there is far more likelihood of success. In 2020 when the COVID-19 pandemic struck, I saw two distinct forms of response in the small business community. For some it was a disaster; for others an opportunity. What I also saw was that those businesses that had owners who tended to be calm, confident, in control of their emotions, physically strong and mentally resilient, were quick out of the blocks. There's a challenge, always, when external change hits us, and it will have emotional impacts. You can be controlled by those feelings or use their energy to harness the opportunity. I know

---

22 Woodward, C. (2005). *Winning: The Path to Rugby World Cup Glory*. Hodder & Stoughton.

which of those two options I saw that worked; I suspect you know which one it was too.

As we have already discussed, building better business really does start by building a better you.

Ways to be strategically you

Today, more than any day that went before it, you have more experience than ever before. Most, perhaps all, of the business that you are building today was designed and created by someone with less experience than you now have. Did they do a good job then? Can you do a better job now?

Here is where the hard work starts. Just like a medical condition it is time to triage what is wrong with the patient, our business. When we look to ourselves and have a strategy for the self, we must take action and then reflect on the impact that action has had.

Ways to be strategic for yourself

1. For emotional awareness: Write down your emotional states every day for a couple of weeks, identify any patterns and triggers that you see and reflect on how they help or hinder you. A journaling application may help if you like to work from the computer.

2. For mental resilience: Write down 50 activities that bring you joy. Do at least one of them every day, particularly if you are feeling depressed or negative, or when something triggers those moods.

3. For physical wellbeing: Find ways to increase the physical activities you enjoy; walking, running, swimming, yoga, etc. all have a part to play. Make time, schedule it so that you do some exercise every day.

6 Skills

The first business strategy

In the business audit I mentioned earlier, out of the four business strategies most respondents rated skills as their strongest. That's not surprising – in fact I'd have been worried if the ratings had shown otherwise, as most businesses are built around the skills of the founder. They generally exist to utilise the skills of the people in the business to add value to the customers of the business.

Yet still, we generally seem to know and accept that there are skills needed for the business that are not easily accessed. The results across a wide range of businesses suggest that most small businesses have access to some, but not all, of the skills they need to achieve their goals.

Let's think about that: nearly all small businesses know for sure that there are skills their business needs but they do not (readily) have access to, nor do they have those skills themselves. That has to be a constraint on the business, and it's why really understanding the strategy around skills is so important for building better business.

Paris

In 1990 I took a trip to Paris with my trusty Olympus OM10 camera and two rolls of 36-image film. Looking back now, it's not unusual for me to take 100 or more shots on a single walk. Here I had just 72 to capture the memory of a week. One morning we walked up to Montmartre and walked past the Abbesses Metro entrance. Abbesses is the deepest station in the Metro system, with the platforms some 36 m below the western side of the Montmartre hill, and opened on 30 January 1913. At the time my intention was to capture the beauty of the canopy. It was designed by Hector Guimard, and is one of only two remaining glass-covered 'dragonfly' entrances, known as édicules. If you haven't seen it, then next time you are in Paris I urge you to go and visit and enjoy its design, both simple and detailed, effective and beautiful, graceful and practical. Smaller than the Eiffel Tower, less imposing than Montmartre, without the grandeur of the Louvre, yet still a jewel in the crown of Paris.

It was a time when you had no immediate feedback on the quality of the image, no insights even as to whether it was in focus (and back then cameras had no automatic focusing; all the settings were manual). At the time the camera was relatively new to me, and I had little experience of taking photographs, finding, as many did, that the cost of film and processing was relatively high. Back in England a few days later I took the film to our local processing laboratory which offered access to the public to do their own darkroom work and developed the latent images on the film. As I switched the light back on having developed and fixed the negative, I held the still dripping strip of celluloid up to the light and I knew in that moment that I had a cracking image.

Then we moved on to printing. So much of what we now do digitally to make changes to the relative balance of light and shade, to correct lens aberrations or other flaws can be done in moments, even on the camera itself, or in Photoshop or similar editing software. Not then. It was done in exposing and developing the paper positive. The wonderful early evening light (by chance I'd hit the golden hour) and the long shadows meant pushing the exposure to highlight the darker details but that risked overexposing some other areas. I remember using my hand as a shield to protect some areas of the image from that, and ensuring that I feathered the edges of that adjustment to make it invisible in the final print. Here was the opportunity to try several times until the perfect image came up in the developing tray.

For me (and imagery is a very personal thing) what I had accidentally captured was a moment of early 90s Paris life. A young woman stepping down the steps into the station, another walking past with typical fashion for the time, two young children rollerskating to the side of the station, graffiti on the station stonework and those long evening shadows. I can still smell the coffee fragrances drifting in the evening air and hear the sound of a Citroën car horn when I look at the image, so evocative of that day.

It was several years before I took another photograph that even came close to the success of that one. Yet what that one did was ignite a flame that burned quietly for years, a flame that told me to keep taking photographs. Over those years I did learn the skills, I learned about apertures and ISO numbers, and shutter speeds and much more. Picking up the knowledge that I needed as a novice. The pictures got better, not all of them, but many. By the early 2010s I was often seen with my camera, and occasionally I would be asked to take photographs for clients and colleagues and friends.

Then something else happened. I mentioned earlier in this book that in 2019 I invested in a course on adventure photography run by Jimmy Chin. I was ready to lift my photography game, and I thought his course would do that. I expected the course to cover the nuances and subtleties one could achieve by using the camera more effectively, or by editing. While some of that did appear in the latter part of the course, most of it was about Jimmy and how he worked, how he thought, how he composed in his mind and about him.

I realised that it was only now, 30 years after 'that' photograph, that I was ready to step up. So much changed from that course, so many areas, not just about photography, but about my whole mindset and readiness to be what I really could be. It was one of the best investments in my own skills that I have ever made.

A different lens

Photographers don't just see the world around them as it is, they see how it can be represented, and how, in a single image, they can crystallise that representation so that we can see it too. In my mentoring work, an ability to see how challenges and opportunities can be represented to clients helps them to make the best decisions. That is using those skills or seeing the landscape and representing the story it tells in a different context. Finding the detail to focus on, defocusing less important elements, using a different lens all need the same imaginative approach.

I see the things going on in businesses that other people do not see. I see the nuance of their skills, the subtlety of their knowledge and the context of their experience. In those areas great opportunities lie and so often the business owner will miss them because they aren't able easily to separate the activity and the detail. As an external advisor I have a different lens, and when they can see things through my lens it lets them crystallise the relevant detail, so that they make a more informed, insightful decision.

This is not a photography book; it's not a book to teach you to become a photographer. I'll leave that to others. I hope what you can see though is how my interest in and gradual development of expertise in photography is also showing up in my mentoring work. Our skills are always linked, even when we cannot see the context. What matters here is the recognition of the importance of all skills, and developing the ones that matter to the point where they become a part of who you are.

Our skills turn up in all the work we do. We bring to bear that which we know, and the context of where we learned them doesn't matter as much as applying them to benefit a specific need.

Questions, questions

An ongoing commitment to improving our skills is extremely important when building better business. It's not just our skills that matter, the other strategies do too, but in the context of this chapter, let's dig into this in more detail and how the Journey to mastery again shows up as the underlying explanation of how to achieve that development.

We need to have the knowledge that backs up our skills. I'm sure, like me, you've seen people with talent who apply that talent without knowledge. Often what they do is brilliantly executed, but because of their lack of knowledge, it's just the wrong thing right now; something that answers a different question to the one faced. With experience of using skills and applying them in different contexts, there's more chance of doing the right thing and doing it well. That experience builds over time. There are all the elements of having to hone and practise and rehearse and use the skills in different ways. In my photography I've learned that my skill is best placed in a particular style of landscape photography. In other areas, portraiture, architecture, still life, I can take a picture, and I can use my skills learned in landscape photography, but I'm not at my best.

I've expanded many of my business skills as a result of the experience of setting up my own business. Doing that challenged me to adapt and grow my skills in order to be building better business in my own business too. Let's look at an example. Earlier in this chapter I shared the results of self-assessments from the building better business audit. That showed that, for many small businesses, the skills gaps are recognised. I spent some time early on in my business, and at intervals throughout its development, asking myself what it was that I was skilled at, and where there were skills gaps, and, importantly, what the impact of those gaps was. Actually, it's really hard to ask yourself the right questions. It took me too long to recognise that this process is best done with a trusted partner. They don't need to understand your business in detail – in fact it's better if they don't, so that they can highlight where your musings are unclear to someone without your knowledge.

The single most important skill I needed for my work, especially when working collaboratively, is questioning. Being able to construct a question that frees people to give an open and complete answer is liberating for the other person. Poor questions constrain us to uninformative, contextually light, short and, perhaps, incomplete answers. Mastering the skill of asking better questions was one of the abilities I recognised that I needed to do for my business. What is it in your business that you are good at, yet being better at it would take the whole business up a notch or several? I'd urge you not to settle, but to seek to master the skill.

When I wanted to master the skill of asking better questions, I came across a book called *A More Beautiful Question* by Warren Burger.[23] It's an extraordinary book. It's a book that describes how to construct questions that free the other person to think much more deeply. I recognised how those 'more beautiful' questions (and the answers from them) could unlock how to be building better business for my clients. There is also an opportunity here to be thinking about the nature of thinking.

On this journey to mastery it is important to have an open mind, to see what until now we have not had eyes to see. One of the biggest blocks to mastery is the tendency we all have, as part of the human condition, to believe what we want to believe, not because we have evidence of their veracity, but because it suits our narrative. When we are in that place it's easy, because of the natural biases for confirmation and the weight we can give to the first solution.

I've reflected on how I have gone about honing the skills I felt worthy of my attention. There's a process that I follow which I want to discuss here so that you can consider it in your context, for your skills and for your development.

To develop any skill, we need to think hard about what we do actually know for sure. So often what we know is built on assumption and supposition, not reality. Why does that happen? Most of the time it's a good working practice. Making

---

23 Berger, W. (2014). *A More Beautiful Question: The Power of Inquiry to Spark Breakthrough Ideas*. Bloomsbury.

realistic assumptions is faster than checking every detail, and our experience and skills can guide us based on past events.

Yet when we ask about what we *really* know, different answers can identify areas where we need to look, to check and to validate. Some of the questions I ask are:

- What are we assuming?

- How do we break those assumptions down?

- Are they true?

- What evidence is there for that truth?

- What are my own personal biases?

Asking these questions meant that while I'm letting my skill development happen almost by osmosis, by letting my mind work on options, I'm also directing it.

I'd like to mention another book here that shifted my thinking about what we know and what is fluff or misdirection. Nate Silver's *The Signal and the Noise*, about the art and science of prediction, is a fascinating book about how you get insights from the data and how you separate it from the noise that's always present in the data.[24] Mastery is many things; one of them is understanding the difference between what is real data and what is spurious.

---

24 Silver, N. (2013). *The Signal and the Noise*. Penguin.

Saying yes and saying no

Honing and developing skills doesn't stop when you get to being good, nor when you are better, not even when you are the best in the world. Arguably it is as one approaches being the best in the world that the need to hone and develop the skills becomes more apparent.

There is an inevitability in this too of course, as someone, perhaps you, puts more time and effort into honing a particular skill they have to let go of doing other things. Making the right choice becomes critical too. (In fact I'd argue that making good decisions is a skill that everyone should hone; we'll come back to that in Chapter 11.)

When I make a choice to say 'yes' to working on a particular skill, I know I am saying 'no' to working on others. In order to make room for improving my skills, I know that I may also need to engage with others who have different skills to take some of my less well-aligned work. Arguably core skills for building better business that we all need are in the areas of delegation and outsourcing.

Any way we look at our own skills shows us that we cannot be everything, cannot do everything. We need to work with others, even in a solo business. We need to collaborate and we need to be effective at doing so.

The process of collaboration

Collaboration is more than just working together on the same project. Business collaboration takes time, effort and energy to make it possible for the essential trust and understanding to develop, but when it's in place, you do more, in a more aligned way, more sustainably. What happens as the collaboration is forming and after it has delivered? I have identified five stages, which can take years or moments to complete, depending on the people involved and their awareness of, and trust with, each other.

Consciousness

Here we become aware of the opportunity, or the imperative, for joint effort.

In 1995 I joined TSB to lead the launch of a new product for the firm. Yet three weeks later, having moved my family and fully committed to TSB, they were bought by Lloyds and the project I was there to run was cancelled. In that moment I became conscious of the need to collaborate with others. I had to identify and use my skills to add value to the ongoing work, or I could not expect to continue to work there.

Conversation

In this stage we are exploring the possibility and starting to build understanding and trust. An idea is just an idea, but through conversation with others the idea can be explored and the ideas improved. As the conversations develop, there is a chance for some of the people involved to recognise the skills and knowledge needed to make things develop further. While not yet collaborating, the conversations allow a trust between participants to develop, and that's essential if we are to move further.

At TSB I entered into many conversations which led to understanding what was needed now the merger had been announced. I began to see where my skills were applicable.

Cooperation

This is the stage of mutual self-interest, when people working together advances them toward their individual goals. It requires trust, and its prime purpose is to test whether the trust is justified. As a result of working together, how you achieve and perform is highlighted. If it goes well then trust is enhanced and working style and practices are both exhibited and observed. Inevitably, you'll also see how others react to stress and challenge, which is vital in collaboration.

Within a few days of the merger, I'd identified the key projects that the senior team was interested in delivering, and was bringing my skills to bear in supporting them.

Collaboration

I believe that collaboration is a state in which everyone acts in harmony with mutually shared goals. Trust is a binding force. As cooperation deepens, longer-term strategic goals become clearer and they align. When everyone knows everyone well, knows their skills and approach, it becomes possible for collaboration to develop. When collaboration really starts, all the people involved know what it is they are all aiming to deliver, and what part they play in making it happen. They don't need coordinating management because they know what they need to do, and in the absence of instruction, they make the right choices. Costs tumble, quality goes up, profits rise significantly.

At Lloyds TSB I was asked to take a leading role in the prime post-merger project and to achieve our goals, to bring everyone together as a cohesive, collaborative team.

Cohesion/community

This is where decision making becomes fully distributed. The goals are embedded so actions and choices align behind shared purpose and culture. Cohesive collaborations can endure for generations. Trust is restorative. Once there is a collaborative group, the development of the relationships doesn't stop; it develops in wider areas much as any friendship will. In the process, there grows a deep understanding between everyone, and a sense of community develops. In that environment, there are new opportunities that develop quickly, mutually. In such communities, great things can be achieved.

Now, years after the Lloyds TSB merger projects completed, years after the businesses were again separated following the banking crises of 2008 and later, many of the people involved are still close. The community remains strong as people who worked together then are still supporting and helping each other.

The cost of coordination

When we look at organisations where there is little or no culture of collaboration, nor a backbone of trust, we find hierarchy and management structures and systems. Those mechanisms enable the organisation to coordinate work and manage outputs. It enables them to achieve, and the best of them to achieve greatness, but they have a cost. Indeed the level of top-down control and the manner in which decision making is focused in specific individuals can often be used as a cultural measure – a trust proxy. The more the organisation demonstrates control being concentrated in a few senior people, the less trust you will find throughout the operation.

Even in smaller units of organisation within a business there can be pointers to the embedded costs of coordinating the work. When we look at projects, as an example, there are usually roles like project or programme manager, whose sole purpose is the coordination of the work and the review and analysis of progress. Decision making is often bottlenecked with these individuals. That always indicates a relative lack of collaboration at a cultural level.

The impact is that the business suffers from a longer and poorer (strategic) decision-making process which takes time to filter down through the organisation and takes longer to evaluate, review and change. The hierarchy itself often means layers of middle managers who aren't productive; rather, they are coordinating and managing those below them on the instructions of those above them. It's very costly, and in the more commoditised sectors can be the difference between a business model that is profitable and bankruptcy.

If there is low trust and little unconscious collaboration, then the hierarchy provides a framework in which organisations can coordinate work and so deliver value to customers, and, despite the costs, it can be the only way to move forward in those situations in the short term.

What's the alternative? When organisations remove the hierarchy, and the costs of coordination associated with that, they have to rely on the productive resources being able to coordinate their work without (significant) overt management. When does this happen? When those doing the work are being mentored by masters and encouraged by each other to make progress. That happens easily when there is a desire for one goal, consistently understood by all, and for decisions and choices to be taken in the spirit of mutual interest, rather than self-interest.

Starlings

These are the features of collaboration, and when an organisation has become truly skilled in creating that sort of cultural framework then the collaborations become cohesive, embedded and mostly unconscious.

Like flocks of starlings creating beautiful patterns in the evening sky, no one conducts the display, yet it remains together and ensures the flock will settle to roost in the most effective way for all of its members. You can't get that, and the benefits of the dramatically reduced costs of coordination, without taking all the steps on the journey of collaboration. This is a big prize, and it's worth setting out to achieve it.

People who are masters of their art don't outsource; instead they create partnerships, they secure a shared commitment to the outcomes, not just a purchased result. Studying what those people who naturally build collaborative relationships really do I've noticed how long it can take to create an enduring collaboration. That's because of attention to the fine detail of building trusted relationships.

The narrow focus that is needed for mastery of a skill highlights the benefits of deepening wisdom. It is something that only the few who make the real effort to know more and more about less and less discover about the core of their work as less-aligned elements of their work are ignored. I've come to realise how the practitioner tends to enjoy their ability to be a bit of a 'Jack of all trades' (and it's no surprise to me that this cliché ends with 'master of none'). To be clear, this is not a bad thing at all – most of the time, most of the population are employed for their skills as practitioners, for their ability to be 'good enough' in most circumstances.

For the master or the aspiring expert/master, this is not enough. That's why they collaborate with others to free themselves from the chains and constraints of having to do many things rather than their *thing*. What is your thing? Where could you take your skills to be world class?

It wasn't until I was really honest about my skills that I could plan what to do. I made lists of what I was good at, what I enjoyed (which was not the same), and what I needed to be exceptional at in the business (again, not the same). I started to see a pattern.

One example was that on my 'good at' and 'enjoyed' list was photography, but it wasn't on my 'needed for the business' list. At least not initially. I realised when thinking this through that I nearly always sourced imagery for the articles and blog posts I was writing. 'What if…' I asked myself, 'What if I could link these two and use my own imagery for the blogs?'

There were other elements on the 'needed for the business' list that weren't on the other lists and so I started to seek out the very best in those fields (not the best I could afford, just the best) to understand the skill and mastery of it. There were times I had to compromise on acquiring the skills because of cost, for sure, but without an understanding of what mastery of that skill looked like it wasn't possible to pick the best practitioner to deliver it. It's a facet of the art of the possible.

As I mentioned earlier in this chapter, if the business, or an individual in it, has to coordinate everything for the skills which they have outsourced, costs can spiral quickly. The time for specifying what is needed, then verifying that the work is being done on time, providing quality assurance and so on can all have an impact on effectiveness. Collaborative partners can be trusted, you have chosen them for the skill, and if you have built the right collaborative relationships then, just like the flock of starlings, the coordination you need will be light, or non-existent.

Ways to be strategic with your skills

1. Write down a list of skills – identify which you are good at, which you enjoy, and which the business needs.

2. For the skills that are on all three lists consider which you want to focus on and improve, seek out the best that is out there and study what they do and learn what you can from them.

3. For the skills that you need for the business that are not the ones you will focus on, find and build relationships to start the collaborations you need to be building better business.

4. These lists evolve, and as a result of writing them out I have made changes to my business model to accommodate the best way to have the best skills available to me. That is what good strategy is for after all!

7 Systems

*I value self-discipline, but creating systems that
make it next to impossible to misbehave is more
reliable than self-control.*

– Tim Ferriss

A part of the whole

My sense is that most small business owners fall into one of
two camps: those who adore systems, processes, automation,
hacks, tricks (whatever you like to call them) and those who
can't get their minds around them.

So let's be clear about what a system is before we go too much
further. The dictionary defines a system as 'an assemblage or
combination of things or parts forming a complex or unitary
whole', and that is a good starting point.[25] When a business
takes a call from a potential customer and adds that person to
a customer relationship management (CRM) database, they are
using a system to record the data, but the act of recording it is
part of a larger system that supports the business's sales efforts.

Some systems are well defined, and we'll discuss how that
helps (and how it can sometimes hinder) later in this chapter.

---

25 'System'. Available at: www.dictionary.com/browse/system, accessed 14/11/2021.

Drawing in a client

Whenever I settle down at my desk, or open my calendars, or email, or pick up a pen, or a phone to talk to a client, I am using some part of a system. It may be a formal, defined, predetermined system, or an informal one. Perhaps the simplest of all is the notebook and pen.

I have a morning routine. I sit down at my desk and write a short journal entry to start my day. For the longest time I didn't really understand the power of journaling, but that opportunity to write whatever comes to mind allows me to get my thinking into a place where I can be more productive. Some days it is a chance to clear out thoughts that distract, acknowledge them on paper and dismiss them. On other days it allows me to develop thinking that either opens my mind to more research or expands on relevant topics that I can draw on throughout the day. After that, I open my calendar. I'm looking for the shape of my day, then I scan my to-do lists and allocate time for the important work. Finally, I step away and make a coffee, which gives me the space to assimilate what needs to be done. When I go back, I'm ready to get on with it. That's my 'getting going' system. Yours will be different, and it should be.

When I set up my mentoring business, I wanted to be sure that my clients all had an experience that met their needs, exceeded their expectations and addressed the things that were important to them. For a long time I described what working with me would be like, but one day, sitting with a prospect, I drew (and bear in mind that my drawing skills are, ahem, weak) a flowchart of the steps we would take if we were to work together. My prospect looked up from the sketch and asked, 'When do we start?'

My prospect recognised that I had a well-thought-through system. They could see that my mentoring wasn't a random collection of conversations. They knew how our work would apply to their business, and in their context in ways they could see would make a significant and rapid difference to them. The system I had developed has been honed and improved over the years, but remains fundamentally the same. I use it every day. That clarity sells, and people are reassured by understanding the flow of a system.

Compromise

Systems are designed to do one of a few things. I think these are the most important:

- creating the time for you to focus on what you love

- unlocking sustainable profits

- reducing risks and uncertainty.

I don't mention in that list anything about technology, software, hardware, process design, checklists and so on. All of these elements can help to support *how* a process is implemented, but none of them can design the process or its purpose. Those elements won't tell you how your customers feel or what their reaction will be.

With so many interlocking systems, there's a real challenge in keeping everything in step, as well as the overhead of the learning curve. That's why I think it is important to focus on the outcomes that are sought and design the overall system before seeking the best tools to help deliver it.

If you are using software to support your business processes, remember that the software will have been written by people working to someone else's specification. The chances of it being a perfect fit for your ideal business system is slim. That means we are going to compromise, and it is better to do that knowing what give and take there has been than simply accepting a compromised system as 'the best we can do'. If you do simply accept it, you won't understand with clarity the full impact of the enforced compromises you have made, and that's why designing the system first is so important.

Your systems start with you – they should free you to be you. To do that, they need to be designed to do it.

Overcoming overwhelm

One of the challenges when a business looks at the various tasks and activities where consistency would be beneficial is that there can be a mountain of work that appears on the to-do list. That's not motivating – far from it in fact. So there is a need to think about starting with a system for systems (and, if you are like me, you'll smile at the 'meta' nature of that).

Overwhelm – that feeling of a tsunami of important work and no real plan to get through it all – is a symptom, not a disease. It's a warning, and it should be heeded. It's a symptom of a lack of a strategy for dealing with a workload that has expanded beyond the resources available to deliver it. In reality, I've not yet met a small business that doesn't have more on its to-do lists than there is time to do them. Every business owner is constantly making choices about what is important and what is not, what can be done, what will be done, and what won't. While overwhelm is a feeling that can get in the way, it is powerfully, destructively self-fulfilling.

Strategically, goals don't change because of a short-term spike in perceived workload. That makes them the touchstone to turn to when overwhelm strikes. Why? Well, they provide the support structure you need to be able to make better decisions. Suppose you had a goal, as I did, to write a book, in my case, this book. I'd signed a contract to provide the manuscript by a particular date. In a period of overwhelm a few weeks before that deadline. the choices about what to do now, what to do later, what to ask someone else to do and what to decline, had a context that made it easier to make an informed decision.

In fact, I had wrapped a system around my decisions. Roughly, in my mind, I was triaging them, deciding what was important and what was not. I had a mental checklist of questions which I ran through (I will come back to checklists shortly):

- What, exactly, needs to be done now?

- What goal will this move me closer to?

- Is it the best way to do that?

- When should it be done by?

- Who else is involved?

- What can they do or tell me to help?

- When does it really need to be done by?

- Who is waiting for this work, and do they need to know anything as a result of this thinking?

It is worth writing down the answers as you may need to revisit the tasks and make further prioritisation decisions later and your written comments will save you vital time. Answering the questions gives you information, and that aids better decision making. Please remember though that when you change your priorities it affects others so do make everyone that needs to know about the changed circumstances aware of them, even if they will be disappointed. That's so much better than letting them down later, when it may be more critical for them.

Noticing difference

Even the absence of a system is a system. Let's take an example. A typical engagement for a business advisor, whether that is a coach, a mentor or a consultant, arises because the customer knows that they could be doing better in some way, and is looking for support to find those ways and implement them.

I recall working with a client who viewed each of his engagements as unique, and that as a result it wasn't possible to 'systematise' what they were doing. I've run across that situation many times. Together, we went through the last four or five times he had been engaged with a new customer and looked at what happened. We looked for similarities – elements that were always the same, elements that were sometimes the same, and those that were always different.

I'm sure you have guessed by now that something close to the Pareto principle was true here. Eighty per cent of the system he applied was the same every time, and 80 per cent of what was left was 'mostly' the same. A small proportion was different. From the point of view of how that feels, however, it's the differences that are noticeable because the elements that are similar become unconsciously competent and habitual.

Roughly speaking (and I'm simplifying here to make the point) the system involves a period of information gathering; a period of analysis; a period of creating advice; and a period of planning. Coaches, mentors and consultants work differently when creating advice. A coach works by exploring with the client what their view is, a consultant offers their expert opinion, and a mentor may use some of both techniques. For each of those high-level elements of the process, it's possible to define sub-processes, and so on. The level of detail needed depends on the business and how it will use the system.

One important point to note here though is that if a business is planning to scale, or to sell, then its systems will have to be operated in future by people who know nothing about those systems today. The more, and the better, that a business documents its systems, the more consistent, scalable, saleable and valuable it becomes.

Shelf life

For a long time now, perishable foods have been given a 'best before' or 'use by' date. 'Best before' dates are about quality; food which is beyond its best before date may have lost some texture or taste, but will generally be safe to eat. 'Use by' is about safety, not quality. It's generally only used on very short shelf-life products and those for which bacteria that cause food poisoning may not be apparent from the smell or look of the product.

In general, a system which works today will work tomorrow, but just like long shelf-life food, the world is changing all the time and your system may gradually stop meeting customer needs as well as it might.

Imagine a business in the 1970s developing a system for communicating with customers via the postal network. It may have given its managers recording devices and had a typing pool of experienced and accurate transcribers. Each letter would then be checked and signed in ink, put in an envelope and sent to the post room to be sent to the customer. Accuracy, brevity, relevance and speed may all have been measures of that system. Would it have the value today that it had then? Would it still be cost effective? Obviously not. That system has probably evolved into one that monitors many channels on social media and email. Automated website communications, SMS response algorithms and FAQs may deal with many customer enquiries with personal intervention when those systems could not solve the customer's needs. It's likely that systems today are more complicated, more integrated, much faster and less personal – but more personalised – than those of the 1970s.

Changing a system could be something that happens when a system fails, but that may happen later than would be optimal. Instead of waiting until the process fails, I recommend having a 'review by' date, rather like a 'best before' date for each system in a business. In my business, I document the major processes in a private wiki, and each has a review date associated with it.[26] My annual and monthly systems are designed to pick up those that need to be reviewed and allow me to schedule the work. As I read that I understand that what I am suggesting here can sound like a lot of extra work, but consistently I find the reverse is true. Evolving systems as they are used and ensuring that they remain as fit for purpose as possible saves me time overall. It's an investment that has, and I am sure will continue to, pay dividends.

Design

In my business, and in all the businesses where there are robust and reliable systems I've seen, there are some common features. Fundamentally these boil down to five elements:

- **Inputs:** ensuring you have what is needed for the system to work (data, software, resources, skills, etc.)

- **Process:** an understanding of the steps to follow – most commonly this is achieved by developing a checklist

- **Outputs**: clarity about what is expected as a result of the system and how quality will be assured

---

26 A wiki is a software system that allows you to create pages and keeps a record of the history of each page. Wikipedia, the online encyclopaedia, is an example.

- **Review**: a willingness to (regularly) review the process without pre-judgement

- **Evolve**: determination to further improve the process based on that review.

It can be insightful to capture tricks and tips as you go. Checklists are useful, but the practical, real-world understanding from those who have undertaken the work is valuable for everyone who has to use the system in future.

Developing instinct

Systems don't make experts, and sometimes, to contradict some of what I have said earlier, they can also constrain rather than free. Good systems mean that practitioners can undertake processes that they have the skills to deliver but have little or no direct experience of. That is, after all, how most businesses bring new employees up to speed with how to do what the business does. Gradually, the experience of following the processes and systems will bring the quality and effectiveness of a new practitioner up to the level of others.

Expertise is about understanding the context of the process and how that context affects it. The subtleties and nuances of how to undertake the steps and the depth of experience allows experts to operate a system that needs to adapt when things aren't quite the same.

Mastery, though, understands the system at a different level. There's real clarity, not just about how to do it, but why that matters and to whom. Bearing in mind that mastery is as much about identity as activity, there's an element of subsuming the system into each individual. It becomes instinct.

Checklists

Checklists come in two guises. First, a checklist that tells you all the steps to perform and which is used in advance; it highlights both the inputs and the actions. An example here is the lists that a pilot will go through before taking off. It's very likely that the pilot knows what to check, but the list ensures that none get forgotten, and when the order of steps is important that it is followed in the correct way.

The second type of checklist is used after the process: it's more of a quality assurance for the process. It checks the actions and the outputs. Some processes will use both types.

When I design a process I prepare both checklists. I have found it is always worth recording what you need to use the system, and where those inputs come from. I also record what to do with the outputs, who needs to know that the system has been completed, and how that will be communicated. After a while, I have a pre-developed, high-level system and often that is enough to guide the work.

As I work through checklists I make notes and capture any tips or tricks that will make it easier next time. It's also worth recording what skills are needed to deliver each step (see previous chapter) in the checklist so that if someone else is following it they know what skills they need.

Systems are dynamic; they change as the world changes, so don't be afraid to break your own checklist, but if you are going to, make sure that you know what it is that causes the change and what you need to do differently. Check afterwards that it gave you the effect you originally sought.

If you would like to dig under the skin of how checklists can support your business (and the various types of checklists that exist) I recommend reading Atul Gawande's book *The Checklist Manifesto*.[27]

Ways to master your processes

1. Start developing your system by creating a checklist, a list of reminders of the steps that need to be taken and the outputs that you seek.

2. Evaluate the best ways to achieve the outputs you want, and identify the compromises you need to make to accommodate any limitations in delivering them.

3. Record any tips and tricks and ideas for improvement every time you run the process, and reflect on it when its review date arrives.

---

27 Gawande, A. (2011). *The Checklist Manifesto: How to Get Things Right.* Profile.

8 Sales

To build a long-term, successful enterprise, when you don't close a sale, open a relationship.

– Patricia Fripp

The lifeblood of business

No business can survive without sales. It's critical to every business that it attracts (the right) customers for the right reasons, and provides them with a product or service which delivers (the right) value for them.

All too often, businesses do have great products that add real value for customers, yet they still fail to make the product a success because they don't have a good sales process. If you are reading this book, you've probably read others about sales, or marketing or communications (we'll come on to that in the next chapter), perhaps some about pricing, or negotiation, and others about mindset and more. Amazon UK lists over 60,000 books in the category of 'sales and marketing' so there's no shortage of knowledge to help explorers become novices. Training courses abound to help novices become practitioners and hone their skills. Yet, when I talk to small business owners, over and over again they cite sales as the area in which they need support.

In the business audit (https://audit.williambuist.com), sales, of all five strategic areas, scores consistently low.

In many ways, it's not a surprise. Small businesses excel at what they do, not necessarily *selling* what they do. It is a different skill (see previous chapter). In business we need to be at least practitioners, if sales cannot be outsourced or delegated.

Why? Because sales are the lifeblood of every business: without a good flow of customers and prospects you will eventually run out of cash. Sales tend to follow a pattern, and when a business understands and optimises the processes that work best for their clients and prospects, sales become predictable and consistent.

People buy what they want, not necessarily what we can see that they need. Think about your own buying habits. I'm sure, if you are like me, there are things you buy which you just like – perhaps it's a brand of pizza, or a type of fruit, or a Mars bar, or whatever your personal preferences are. I don't *need* that brand of pizza, it's just the one I *want*. When I am taken to a different brand, it's because I've been sold it with advertising, or by necessity (my favourite is not available). What if we see something like the first tablet device? Do we need it? The vendor may know that the product can give us greater efficiency, and if that is what we seek then we may want to buy it even though our current needs are being met. We are persuaded by marketing, advertising and conversations that make us desire it. Once we want the product badly enough, we'll buy it, and then we find out how much we need it (which can vary from not at all to finding it essential).

That distinction is important, of course, because we filter the conversations with our knowledge and skill and experience. That means we will see areas where our skills will make a difference. For our prospect, however, there may not even be an awareness of the possibility, let alone an ability to recognise how it might apply in their context. Where there is clear value in the sale, we should design our offer to satisfy the client's wishes while delivering the solution they need.

Why did they buy?

For some people, sales is a way of life: they love the thrill of the chase, the rush of emotion when a prospect either says 'yes' or 'no'. Perhaps that is you? For others, it is a drudge – something that their business needs but they personally hate, yet it is an important part of their role. Perhaps that's you? I've felt both the drudgery and the thrill along the way. Both are symptoms of sitting as a practitioner at best.

It took me rather longer to realise something about sales than it should have done. I was in a conversation with a potential client; a conversation that had gone well, and I could see that they were interested. Yet I also knew I had not won and would not win the deal. Has that ever happened to you?

I spent some time thinking about what I was doing in those sales conversations, and why they weren't working. In simple terms I could see how what I did would make a real difference to the prospect's business. After a few mentoring sessions they would have clarity of vision and take decisions with more certainty. The result of that would be more, better clients, who get a better, more aligned result and sang the praises of my prospect to their networks.

It was obvious that they needed the help. The trouble was, they didn't want it – at least not how I was describing it. Emotionally, I was way off the mark. I needed to change my approach to work with my prospect's emotions, rather than my own. I also recognised that I was letting my cognitive biases (mostly confirmation bias and first-solution bias – see page 181) stand in the way of the realities of their desired outcome. 'Not there,' I was saying. 'Don't go there, come here with me,' but I wasn't leading them to that conclusion in a way that made them want to move. I discuss cognitive bias in more detail in Chapter 11.

It's the wrong message, isn't it? Better instead to think about what they want and then react. 'Wow you want to go there, that's great! Here's how I/my product/my service can make that happen for you!' In other words, sell people what they want, emotionally, and then give them what they need, rationally.

I started examining my sales process and realised that I really didn't even know what my existing customers had wanted when they had decided to buy what I do. They had bought what I had sold them and I knew exactly what that was, but I was making all sorts of assumptions about what they had wanted, starting with the obvious one. Because they had bought what I knew they needed, I assumed that they had wanted what they needed. I checked; they didn't.

I reached out to my present and past customers and asked them this question: 'I know what I sold you, but what did you want and what did you get?' The answers I got were highly informative and some distance away from what I thought they would be. It was an enlightening time. Next time you speak to a client, ask them that question and then listen to the answers, pay attention to them, and think about how you can use that information to help a future discussion with a similar prospect.

Open the relationship

While this is not a book about how to 'do' sales in your market, it is a book that includes some thoughts about the strategy of selling that will focus your efforts in your own context.

One of the things I've observed over the years is how businesses can miss an opportunity when they open a sales conversation with a new prospect. The first is that they treat it as opening a *sales* conversation, and so preface their interaction with all the things that (traditionally) go with selling. There's a tendency to want to have a discussion about the product or the service too early in the conversation. In the strategy for sales that I discuss shortly, you will see how there is a need to be relationship, not outcome, focused. That's even more true in a small business, where the relationship between the buyer and your business has your personality rippled through it.

Don't try to close the deal; instead, open the relationship. My good friend and fellow speaker, Patricia Fripp, whose quote opens this chapter, is adamant that business is all about the relationships you build and the connections and support those relationships give to you. The sales will follow if you trust the process, step back from forcing the pace and have the right attitude. If you do, the quality of your sales and their value to both you – and your new clients – will improve rapidly.

The perfect decision

Let's explore a strategy for sales. What is your goal? For me, and perhaps for you, I wanted to develop a strategy that provided a consistent, reliable, controllable flow of business. I wanted a strategy that I could turn up or down as I needed. It took a while, and there were some missed steps along the way. Bear in mind as you read the next section that my business is an advice business, and these strategies work well in that environment, but they may need to be modified for yours. My intention, in these pages, is to give you a starting point from which you can evolve your own sales strategy.

Stephen Covey, in his seminal work, *Seven Habits of Highly Effective People*, tells us that one of the habits is to 'Seek first to understand, then to be understood', and that is our starting point too. I developed six strategic aims for sales:

1. **Understand what potential clients want for their businesses.** This requires us to ask the right questions and listen to the answers without judgement. While that sounds easy, in reality it's hard, and requires a honing of skills (see previous chapter) and lots of practice.

2. **Show how their 'want' can be met by what is available in the market.** That's about identifying the links and understanding how your prospect could meet their desired outcome. This is important because it helps you to see the world from their point of view, and see the alternatives that they have laid out in front of them. Remember, one option is to stick with the status quo, too.

3. **Support the buyer in making an informed choice.** How often do we make a decision to make a big purchase, but put it off? For most major purchases (cars, houses, consultancy) we look and then reflect for a while before committing. New questions arise and need to be answered. Validating desire against practicality and so on, all have a part to play. So when we are supporting our potential buyer, we need to be a trusted partner, answering the questions without a vested interest in the outcome. Sometimes, you'll help them decide to use a competitor or do nothing, but if that is the right decision for them the trust you build will be invaluable in your future relationship with that prospect. (In addition, it adds value for all the people they talk to about how you helped them reach the right decision.)

4. **Be fair about price.** Your business is your business. Its costs and overheads need to be met by the income you generate, and from your buyers' perspective, the purchase of your product should always give them more value than it costs. Being fair about charging means really understanding both sides of the financial decisions and balancing cost and reward in a fair way for everyone. In the sales process talking about budgets and the buyers' expectations is always informative. Your prices communicate many things, not just the money. Your pricing is a reflection of how you value your own work, and buyers recognise that. That's why seeking sales by lowering price rarely works for anyone.

5. **Be the right person for them.** In all the discussions and understandings, find out first if you are the right person to deliver to them (if you aren't and you know a better person, make the introduction). If you are, give them the information to reach that conclusion, and then – and only then – discuss the details of how you will help and how that will meet their desire.

6. **Be the only person for them.** If you are the right person, find out what would make you stand out from everyone else that they have worked with and build that into what you do. This is where mastery really works to your advantage, but even while you are on the journey, think hard about the knowledge, skills, experience and insights that set you apart.

All of these strategic aims require listening deeply and giving the buyer time to think and assess the information you are providing. My overarching strategy is not for sales, but to support buyers in making the perfect decision for them. I've learned over the years that if a buyer knows you will give honest, informed, non-judgemental advice to support them, they will come back to talk to you often, and when the time is right for what you do, they will buy quickly.

Master salespeople

I decided it would be useful to study those for whom sales is what they do, and who have become masters of their art. The more I looked, the less selling I saw. Those who have become master salespeople for their business don't really sell.

They create opportunities for those that want (there is that word again) to buy. There's a wisdom in mastery that gives people confidence in their own ability and certainty that when the fit is good, their prospect will buy. There is also certainty that when the right person is in front of you, making an informed choice, that their choice will be the right one, whatever their decision is. Not being emotionally attached to the outcome but ensuring that your prospect makes a fully informed choice without pressure to fall into any one particular outcome is, in my experience, the most powerful way to win business. Just remember to ask them to make the choice when the time is right. Mastery is about knowing, every time, when the time is right.

Honing the sales skills

In my work with clients, and as I mentioned at the top of this chapter, sales is the area most often reported as weak. And yet it is also the area where I see most resistance to change in the businesses I work with. I believe that is because the sales function is one that the business owners are relatively inexperienced in. There's a natural feeling that, as novices or practitioners, it feels weaker than the core competence of the business. Bearing in mind that being earlier on the journey to mastery means needing to hone the skills and gather experience. The first strategy, then, is to do more selling, and learn from what is working and what is not.

The strategies I have outlined do not always seem intuitive, and certainly don't feel urgent enough when there is a pressing need for clients today. (Yet, if that is the case, you probably haven't been strategic for some time.)

There are tactics that can solve an urgent need, but they depend on circumstances – the strategies don't. If you aren't using the right strategies for your business, if you are having sales conversations rather than building relationships and recognising desire then changing your strategy will be effective and create lasting and resilient improvements. Not immediately, but soon.

Ways to master your sales strategy

1. Be curious about what your ideal clients want, and develop your approach to explore and develop a reputation for being interested in them.

2. Build a pipeline of relationships (as opposed to prospects) and make a point of nurturing those relationships regularly (you will need a good system to do that well).

3. Follow the six strategic steps detailed earlier in this chapter ('The perfect decision') to support your sales activity in all the relationships that you have built.

9 Signposting

Good writers are in the business of leaving signposts saying, Tour my world, see and feel it through my eyes; I am your guide.

– Larry L. King

Last but not least

The last strategy that every master in business understands and knows needs to be delivered well is signposting. This includes marketing, but also customer communications, internal and supplier messaging and any other information exchange with others.

When we are building better business all our communications are important. Without great marketing we don't attract the right people to us; when they become customers, if the information that we provide isn't good enough, they don't get the value that we promised. If suppliers don't understand (the relevant parts of) our goals and ambitions, how can we expect them to deliver to us for our business to be at its best?

Where are you?

It was very early in the morning. I pulled the car door closed and heard that satisfying clunk. I took a sip of coffee from my travel mug. Turning the key, the car burst into noisy life and I headed toward the motorway. As I approached the motorway junction, the blue squares highlighted that I could turn west toward Wales or turn east toward London. I was travelling to Basingstoke from Chepstow, so I went east.

In a few miles I reached the junction with the M5. Signs a mile or so back had alerted me to the upcoming junction; now the overhead choices were London, The MIDLANDS and The SOUTH-WEST. I noticed that the regional words in the sign were capitalised and the font was big enough to be read even when travelling fast. I stayed on the M4 and the miles gradually rolled by. The signs told me as I passed first Bristol, then Bath, then Chippenham and Swindon, but still no mention of my destination. It was one of those journeys where large parts of it passed without any real consciousness of the details.

At Newbury I turned off the motorway and onto the A34. The first mention of Basingstoke came even later, on route signs from the A34. Gradually, they became more prominent as I neared my destination. In Basingstoke itself I found the smaller direction signs and ultimately the name of the road, in small black-on-white print, that told me I had arrived.

It wasn't important to know every detail of the journey. I didn't even need to know exactly where I was (although that is a point I will return to). I did need to know two things, and only two, and that is what the signposts provided. I knew I was on the right road, and I knew I was going in the right direction.

Of course, I knew my destination when I set out, and that was in mind when I was mentally checking what the signposts were telling me.

Margaret Calvert

Those signs are no accident. They evolved and developed from the work of a relatively unsung hero of design, Margaret Calvert.[28] Calvert is responsible for many of the pictograms that have been used on road signs in the UK (and subsequently adopted beyond). Perhaps the most familiar one we all see today is the road works sign! Calvert, along with her colleague Jock Kinnear, is also responsible for the development of the Transport typeface.[29] This font has been adopted by many countries around the world, so effective is it at communicating the right information at the right time.

The key to the success of the typeface is legibility, so that a driver can take in, in a split second, the information that they need. The key to the success of road signs is not just legibility but also brevity. Just what you need to know, just when you need to know it.

Have you ever called the police to report a problem or an accident on the motorways (as a passenger of course…)? In the conversation they will ask you to read one of the half kilometre marker signs – these have the road designation, a number and a letter (e.g. M4, 121.6 A). They are always on the left, and they provide positional information from an origin point, so my example here is 121.6 km away from the origin of the M4 – London. This would tell the emergency service where and in which direction I am travelling, if I needed to get them the information. Brevity, again, makes it much more likely that the right information is passed at the right time. On posts

---

28 'Margaret Calvert'. Available at:https://en.wikipedia.org/wiki/Margaret_Calvert, accessed 30/03/2021.
29 'Transport (Typeface)'. Available at: https://en.wikipedia.org/wiki/Transport_(typeface), accessed 16/04/2021.

every 100 m, on the hard shoulder, the distance and direction letter are also printed. These can't be read while travelling but are there for motorists who have broken down.

Of course, road signage has continued to evolve, particularly as traffic volumes have increased. When Calvert and Kinnear were developing signage, the volume of traffic was much lower (and average and maximum speeds higher) and it was possible to put all the signage to the left of the carriageway. As traffic volumes built up around certain routes, it became necessary to have some signage overhead to ensure that it could be seen. More recently, dot matrix and LED screens provide more detailed information. I'm personally not sure that Calvert would have thought these a welcome addition, but in situations where traffic speeds are significantly reduced, providing additional information is helping drivers to understand the likely impact on their journey.

The right information, given in the right way, with both clarity and brevity, makes it possible for a driver travelling quickly to both absorb and process it with certainty and then for them to take action, the right action, to complete their journey.

Keeping up the pace

When I think about how I behave when I feel like I am off track, I can see some common factors. Those common factors turn out to be important for business. Have you ever felt lost while driving somewhere? (Perhaps less so since the advent of satellite navigation, but still…) If you are like me you'll slow down, search for more information from the landscape, and if still there is uncertainty, maybe pull over and consult a map. The pace of everything slows down, even stops. In business too, uncertainty saps momentum. The right signpost at just the right time can make all the difference to the comfort of the journey.

Strategic signposts, in a business context, are thought-through communications, designed for and used at every stage of the process of operating the business. From the moment a new prospect first sees the business to the ongoing follow-up with past clients whose projects are long finished, there is clarity. As a result of that clarity, they know you have thought through this communication and made it relevant and consistent for them. Clients see your branding, style, accessibility and approach. Consequently, they trust your professionalism. They trust you and your business. Naturally, that helps them to make the right decisions faster, more reliably, and with purpose.

Working out what to put on which signpost was something that Margaret Calvert and her colleagues spent a great deal of time testing on both the Preston bypass and the M1. Recognising that drivers only have a moment to absorb the information meant choosing the right information was critical. I would suggest that, in our businesses, we face exactly the same challenge when we are seeking to get information to our prospective customers. Increasingly our world is one in which there are many competing pressures for our attention, so it is vital that we too spend time thinking about what we need to communicate, to whom, and when.

Great expectations

Great signposts give you clarity on where you are going. The signs you provide for others give them the clarity they need. That clarity in communication and direction inspires confidence, not just in the moment for what they seek then, but also confidence that you will continue to provide that clarity and certainty as you work together. I cannot emphasise enough how what you do when you are not being paid by a client colours what they learn to expect when and if they decide to enter into a commercial contract. That's why the experience of your early signposts when they are learning about your business is so important.

Many, perhaps most, disputes have at their heart a breakdown of understanding of the expectations between the people involved. It is vital, truly vital, in building better business, that we set the right expectations *and continue to meet them*. That is the essence of good signposting.

Your business can stand up to the rough patches – every business has them – when you continue to gauge your direction, confirm where you are, and take the right action. Your clients will keep coming back to you for what you do if they know, from your signposts, where they are, with clarity, certainty and confidence.

Are the signposts you need clear to you? Are the ones you give others clear to them?

The right moment

I realised early in my career that the people I admired were not the ones that were desperate to show off how much they knew, but the ones who knew what I needed to keep me moving. These special people provided just enough information to keep my momentum up, and when I needed more information, or some coaching through the development of a skill, they were there again. Again, with just the right information.

This is the skill that comes with mastery. Practitioners often feel a need to demonstrate that they have the knowledge, skills and experience to do the work, and will tend to go into detail quickly. Experts too can seek to reinforce their expertise. Masters know that is counterproductive. Indeed, part of the way we know a master when we see one is how little they share, but how valuable what they share is. One thing, maybe two – not a destination, but a nudge. The right road, the right direction. Nothing else is needed.

That, though, is very hard. It takes skill and insight to know what to say and when to say it, to get that precisely right and to know that it has been received in the right way. It's drawn from experience in part, but also from a knack for recontextualising.

The key to modern signposts is the ability to communicate precisely the information that the driver needs at that moment; nothing more, nothing less. They also make the recognition of information effortless. The eyes can glance at a sign and in a fraction of a second gather the information that is needed therefore freeing the driver to concentrate fully on the road. I suspect that the development of the Transport typeface and the work done in terms of colours and signage and size have, over the years, saved many lives.

Our prospects need information about the products and services we offer, but if we overwhelm them with too much information they will go elsewhere. As they learn about our products and services they need different information; as they approach the decision to buy, we need to guide them with increasing detail, and yet remain with that information in bite-sized chunks. The question I pose when I'm considering marketing my products and services is a simple one: 'What does my potential customer need to know *right now*?' That is the essence of a good communication strategy.

Signposting, though, is not just an activity to undertake as part of the sales process, as marketing for the business. As soon as a prospect has agreed to work with us then they need additional information, reassurance that they have made a good decision. There's a golden hour or two when they are excited about the decision, but it is likely that some questions and doubts will remain. They may need to know how to pay us or to have details of a meeting, the agenda for a mentoring session, pre-course work and so on. Signposting works at every level of the business from identifying a prospect to long after they have signed up.

Throughout the time we are working with a client, we also signpost many elements to them, and the same principles apply. We should provide just the information they need to know so that they continue to know that they are on the right road and travelling in the right direction. With our suppliers, we need to agree upon the destination that we seek (that's about sharing our goals and mission) and then provide the right signposts for them to know they are working with us in the right way too.

There are others too: the regulators, tax authorities and government all require us to provide information at appropriate times. The business communities in which we operate, in networks and our relationships with referral partners and advocates – all need the right signposting.

I think this is the essence of mastery of communications. You know that you are in the presence of a master when their contributions to the conversation are utterly on point, with the beauty of brevity and a conviction borne of wisdom. They provide us with precisely the information we need at precisely the moment we need it and, in doing so, nudge thinking forward so that the journey of understanding of the group as a whole progresses smoothly.

From a practical point of view, how do we go about working out where we need a signpost and what we should put on it?

I recommend starting at the end, rather than the beginning. When we think about our road trip and start from the beginning, it's inevitable we will think about all the things we will need to know throughout the journey. That makes it very likely that we will mistime the information. Instead, if we start at the end then we can think about the journey quite differently. If I am visiting a friend at 26 Downs Lane then, when I arrive, I need to be able to see the house number and not much else.

Now take one step back. As I drive the last few yards, I'm looking for a sign that tells me Downs Lane. The nameplate at the end of the road does that. It's information that comes at a different time to the house number. In our sales process too, we shouldn't be directing people to the signature page without showing them the rest of the contract first.

When I am mentoring clients I suggest that they start designing the sales process in the same way, starting from the moment the client signs the contract, by asking 'What information did I just provide to make that possible?' and then working back through the process.

In my business, when someone decides to work with me, at the point they make that commitment they've most often been seeking information about the practicalities of working together – questions like 'What happens if I have to move a session?' and 'When do I need to make payment and to what account?' are common. So this final meeting is the time to have that information available – it's not needed before.

Then I think about what brought them to that meeting. What information did they need in order to consider it worthwhile? What decisions had they already taken to decide to meet at all? Again, answering those questions requires thinking about what information I need to provide, in what format and when.

By working all the way back to the point when someone first comes across you, perhaps on a webpage, or via a blog or an article, you can see what information is needed then, and what will be provided later. Even on our roads, there's a little bit of forward planning; while the main signs provide details of direction (The SOUTH-WEST) they also provide a frisson of anticipation (Bristol) by alluding to what is going to come next on the journey. Next perhaps, not every staging post. Businesses should do the same.

Take the third exit

It's also an exercise to undertake for your customer and supplier interactions. When working on important communications, or when I catch myself being overly verbose, there are three questions I use to guide me, for clarity, brevity and efficiency:

- **Clarity:** What do they really need to know now?

- **Brevity**: What's the shortest way to express that information effectively?

- **Efficiency:** What is the best medium to use?

I personally find each of these questions difficult to answer. There are some common guidelines that seem to work best in most situations.

On the clarity question, the challenge is not to include extra detail 'just in case'. Instead, include a signpost showing how to get more information if questions remain.

On the efficiency question, a spoken conversation will always be more efficient than a written one, so use writing only when a spoken conversation cannot take place. It can be worth putting important spoken conversations into writing for the record after the conversation concludes. That has the additional advantage of validating mutual understanding and agreement. It's not something that needs to be done every time you have a spoken conversation as it is context dependent, but if in doubt it is best to confirm in writing.

On the brevity question, removing filler words entirely can make a communication sound brusque or overly direct, but too many can sound patronising and woolly. Satellite navigation tends to get this about right. 'At the roundabout, take the third exit' is, in my opinion, better than both 'Take the third exit' or 'When you arrive at the next roundabout, please indicate to turn right, and then, when the road is clear, take the third exit.'

The best business communications tend to be brief but contextual, informational more than directive and as unambiguous as possible.

Ways to master signposting

1. Map out your communications journey from the end back to the beginning.

2. Use the clarity, brevity and efficiency questions to plan the signposts you need.

3. Evaluate the effectiveness and adapt the signposts based on what you find.

Section 3

Mastering Joy

There's no point having great strategies if they don't free you to enjoy what you decide to master, and if that mastery itself doesn't give you joy. In this section we take a look at the impact of mastery on the world and on you. We will conclude by looking forward at how the realisation of mastery can impact you, your identity and what you do.

We'll explore your wider impact and how you can apply your mastery in this section:

1. We'll examine some examples of making a difference in Chapter 10 (page 163).

2. Our best results will always be when the work is undertaken with our full attention behind it, and we will cover that in Chapter 11 (page 175).

3. Mastery isn't just about what you do, but how you work collaboratively to leverage and magnify your impact and how you pass it on. That's in Chapter 12 (page 187).

4. It's important to maintain your individuality, and that's covered in Chapter 13 (page 201).

5. Finally, in Chapter 14 (page 209) we look forward to what you can do next, in order to become a master in your chosen field.

10 Making a Difference

In the beginner's mind there are many possibilities; in the expert's mind there are few.

– Shunryu Suzuki

One dent at a time

This section is called 'Mastering Joy' because, for me, this is a really important part of what motivates me to support my clients. When I speak to them, it is a major motivator for them too. I wondered if this was the general view of most businesspeople, or simply something that reflected my personality and the people who work with me. While it is by no means a scientific study, I asked my wider network via social media, 'What is it about your work that gives you the greatest joy?'

The replies fell into three broad categories. First, there was a group who were motivated by the personal outcomes for themselves, their own impact. That might be the money that their work generates or the appreciation of their clients. A second group were interested in the relationship, focusing predominantly on how the way they worked enhanced and encouraged their joint relationship to deepen. The third group focused entirely on their clients and the impact they were having on others as a result of their work. A few of them were even looking beyond that, to the impact their clients' work was having.

I would suggest the difference between these three main groups is the result of where they are on the journey to mastery. novices and practitioners typically focus on what they do and take great pride in it, and rightly so. They are motivated by what the work does for them, and it seems to me that, for many of them, their ability to deliver the work and do it well (and move on to the next client) is the primary motivation. Practitioners are measuring their success by the personal feedback they get from their clients and their salary or the payment of an invoice.

As expertise develops there is naturally more focus on the relationship. The work is no longer just about achieving the outcome; it's also about providing the client with your knowledge, skills and experience. In nearly all cases when working with an expert, the relationship is critical to that expertise being effective. So it's hardly surprising that what brings an expert joy is the nature of the relationship itself, and the evidence that the relationship is both strong and improving.

As people move toward mastery, the mind shifts toward reach. Not just about how they can use that expertise to help an individual but how they can bring their skills, experience and insights to bear more widely. They want the client relationship to reach far beyond itself. Comments in the responses to my question included phrases such as, 'I love hearing their successes', 'Saving lives and changing behaviours' and 'Sparking epiphanies'. These all point toward reaching beyond the boundaries of the work that has been done.

Most of the businesses I've worked with have expressed a strong intention to 'make a difference'. If we are to actually make a difference, we need to go further than just the expression of the intention. We will talk more in the next chapter about how to go about taking effective intentional action. For now, let us recognise that there is something unique about businesses that have mastered their art. They are rare, but those that do reach further and are influencing and improving the future for others.

I recall working with a training business called Speak First, whose owners had developed a successful business but wanted to do more. They formed a foundation and committed to making financial contributions from the operation of the training business. The foundation undertook work in areas of the world where support for learning would change the lives of people, perhaps for generations to come. One example of the work they undertook was to build floating classrooms in Bangladesh, where children were unable to be educated in the monsoon season because of flooding.[30] We will explore this in a little more detail shortly, but first some context.

For me, it's this reaching beyond the immediate environment of the business itself to change lives for others that is the essence of making a difference. In her wonderful book, *The Power of Onlyness*, Nilofer Merchantdiscusses the importance of making a 'dent' (Nilofer's shorthand for making a difference – a specific meaning for each of us in the world as we each see it).[31] Nilofer understands the nature of making a significant change in the world, and the importance of building a community of like-minded people as a team to deliver, magnify and accelerate the delivery of that change. She concludes the book by saying 'I want you to see that you can redesign what

---

30 'The Floating School in Bangladesh'. Available at: https://blog.speak-first.com/the-floating-school-in-bangladesh, accessed 03/05/2021.
31 Merchant, N. (2017).*The Power of Onlyness: Make Your Wild Ideas Mighty Enough to Dent the World.* Viking.

we do and how we do it, so that we enable the full power of onlyness. You will dent the world to include the best ideas. And, together, dent by dent, we'll reshape the world.'

I've realised that the people who consistently make a dent have become masters of the thing they do. It seems as though it's a prerequisite, and if you are intent on making a difference but have not yet reached mastery in your market, then that is where you should focus. Mastery is an enabler of change, a lubricant to its ease, and the glue that holds a community of change agents and advocates to act in unison. Together, the community can draw on your mastery to spread the value of the work as far and wide as possible.

It is my hope that, together with that knowledge, and your determination, you can and will think more broadly about how your influence can shape the future for all of us and for good.

Lightbulb moments

In my own journey, I've realised how little I was able to make a difference in the early stages of either my career in the insurance industry or within my own business. This is not for my lack of desire, nor an intention to focus on creating value in either of those two careers, but in the reality that, while I was mastering both, I could not focus beyond my own development. On the path to making a dent, one first must become at least expert in what you do, because at that point you're in a position to see how your skills and experience and knowledge can be applied in other areas. The areas where your unique skills do truly make an enduring difference.

As a small footnote to history, one of the reasons I chose to leave my insurance career was the realisation that I would not be in a position to make the sort of difference that was my calling. Today, in a different world, I can reach out and start to see how the final third of my life can be devoted to the difference that I have always wanted to make.

Steve Jobs, then CEO of Apple, in his commencement speech to Stanford University, opined about our inability to join the dots looking forward, and yet when we reflect on the journeys we have actually taken the connections are clear and sharp. Looking back now I can see how my experiences at university, in the development of a deep understanding of uncertainty, ambiguity and risk in the world, and the fascination with cooperation, collaboration and community developed long before I started my business. They have played a vital role in its ongoing development. But I can also see how my experiences since starting my business and working with other business owners have shaped my determination to create a more effective, more efficient, more joyful opportunity for us all.

In my work with business owners, I get the marvellous opportunity to learn about their journeys too. I have the pleasure of seeing them identify their dots and join them together. Collaboratively we can identify the path they have been following. Once those paths are clear then by extrapolating the general direction of travel we can start to see the possible destinations they could achieve. It's deeply satisfying when goals and ambitions line up with the direction people have been, often unaware, travelling on for some time. If the goals of the business and its direction of travel aren't aligned it can be hard to see from the inside; it needs the journey to be seen from the outside for it to be clear. You know it's happening in the 'lightbulb moments' of insight and I nearly always observe an acceleration in the business, and significant reduction of stress too. Your business may not be heading where you think it is, and if it isn't, you will never have the insights you need for mastery.

Uncovering insight

In the work I do with clients we are examining the knowledge that has been gathered since they were first explorers around the topic of what they do. We also see the skills that they have first developed as novices to become practitioners. Finally, we review the experience that they have had along the way that is making them experts. What happens when we do this in a structured, exploratory way is that insights, often new and liberating insights unlock understanding and wisdom. As we have discussed in section one of this book, it is from these insights the true mastery can develop.

In general, but not exclusively, those insights tend to simplify. They are bringing together ideas and thoughts that derive from different parts of the learning journey. For example, knowledge gathered when experience was low is interpreted differently from the same knowledge when experience is more extensive. The process surfaces what has become unconscious competence. As a result, you are able to pass on the knowledge, skill, experience to others more easily. In general, these valuable insights also help you to be building better business every day.

Underneath all that is the reality that every business owner must face. The reality that they are building better business *for something*. For some it may be in order to generate the financial security that they seek, but in my experience this is actually quite rare. More common is about building a shared purpose among the people involved in the enterprise. About doing what they do as well as possible.

For some though the reason to be building better business is in order to make a difference beyond the business. To create wealth, a wealth of opportunity, a wealth of ideas. It is as a result of this sort of thinking that Speak First have been able to build floating classrooms in Bangladesh, and other similar initiatives being undertaken by businesses.

So what?

One question that comes up, time and time again, in these reflective sessions is why something matters. Why does what we do, what each of us is mastering, affect us emotionally as well as practically (financially, operationally, etc.). Speak First didn't build floating classrooms because they needed to be built, although obviously they did, nor because they wanted to sell their products or service, although it may help. They did it because they saw children being deprived of an education that would give them choices in life that too many are denied. In other words a purpose that is far bigger than the underlying rationale of the business itself.

As I talk to others I consistently see the most passionate action is aligned to personal goals and beliefs. No surprise there of course, but there also seems to be a correlation between what is important in the business with what people put time, effort, energy and money into, beyond the business. For masters, what they think about as important in their lives is always what they know to be important in the lives of others. For those that aspire to be masters that knowledge makes it both possible and easy to put the effort in to make things happen.

Models

If you want to be the best you can be, someone building better business, who wants joy from that, and wants to make a difference for others, then there is an underlying truth. Those three elements can happen together for you if there is an underlying mastery of the work that you do. Without that depth of insight, experience, skill and knowledge, there is going to be frustration that kills the joy, sometimes, perhaps all the time. Without it, the business cannot always be moving on an upward trajectory. Without it, it won't be possible to make that wider difference significant enough.

We have acknowledged throughout the pages of this book that mastery is not simply the extreme end of expertise. It is also about narrowing the range of things you do down to an essence of what you do extraordinarily well. Niching is important, but it's the narrow part of the egg-timer: as mastery develops so you widen again your understanding of the context that your work can be applied to. You learn the skills and gather the experience from the specific things you work on, but mastery gives insight that allows one to see beyond the niche to the more general application. That's why masters sometimes develop 'models': ways to explain their insights, in the general rather than the specific sense. Models simplify complex ideas or processes. They provide a framework to give others knowledge when they do not yet have sufficient experience or skills to apply on their journey.

When it comes to making a difference, it is that general case that allows businesses like Speak First to apply their insights. They have specialist knowledge and honed skills in training, and their experience of sharing knowledge with others and understanding the importance of the environment in which they do the work all have a bearing. These insights are not trivial;

they have depth and multiple facets. When there is an issue with the environment, their mastery can make connections to see solutions in a different way. The monsoon season on the flood plain of a river delta in a world where global warming is increasing the frequency and severity of rainfall and raising sea levels needs new solutions. Recognising that education changes the future – not just for children, but for their descendants too – Speak First know the environment matters deeply. Creating both the physical environment by building floating classrooms and the education environment by supporting the teachers who will use them makes lasting and profound change. I have no doubt that, had the leaders of Speak First not achieved levels of mastery in their endeavours, they would have been mired in running the business, and too focused on it to have the insights they needed to make the time, find the energy and put the focus on the greater work they have done.

As a quick aside, I don't want to leave the impression that there is a kind of nirvana here, that once you reach mastery you'll be graced with unlimited energy and time to do this wider work. The world will continue to throw curve balls at you; no business was untouched by the SARS-CoV-2 virus that caused the COVID-19 pandemic that started in late 2019. Mastery can't protect you from risk after all, but what it can do is mitigate the risks; those who have mastered the key element or elements of business don't get thrown off course easily, because of the insights that mastery brings.

A piece of paper

Another aspect of what I've learned by working with business owners is that some of what they do as a result of building better business is a surprise. How you will make a difference may well surprise you when you realise what you will do.

The opportunity to make a difference doesn't come neatly packaged up, delivered by Amazon with an instruction book. Something will frustrate you, something will be less than perfect, something will be big enough to make you lose sleep, or cheer, or shout in anger from the rooftops. Perhaps not today, maybe not tomorrow, but one day. When it does, listen to those emotions.

You will recall in Chapter 5 that we discussed emotional awareness, and I think that is why it is important to really hone those skills as part of a strategy of mastery. It's why I recommended practising understanding emotions and triggers for them. By becoming proficient at that, and making it a habit, it becomes part of your own self-mastery. You'll recall I said I don't believe that one can master a topic until one has mastered one's emotional connection to it.

When the right thing comes along, the opportunity to make a difference along with the recognition that you can make that difference (or facilitate it) because of what you have mastered, then you should be ready to grab it. That means preparation.

The insight here is that it's always difficult to prepare for something that you cannot yet describe, and may not even yet know. That skill, too, is one that you should hone.

When I was working as head of the risk management department for Lloyds TSB Insurance working out how to prepare for events that we did not know, could not describe and might not see until they had happened was a big part of the job. In the end I realised I was using a simple process to think it through. This is not a book on risk management, it's a book about building better business, so I'll not dig into the risk management theories. I'll just distil the essence of the process, adapted to identifying how you can make a difference rather than as a risk management tool. This is another example of how mastery works – it allows us to learn a skill in the narrow confines of a niche activity and then use what we learned in the general case.

First you need to activate awareness so that your mind makes the connections it needs to when you are looking for the opportunities. I'm sure you've experienced the impact of making a big purchase – say a car – on your awareness. You don't see many of the brand or model you want until you decide to buy it, and then you see them often. It's not that there are suddenly more of them, just that your awareness has been activated. That's the sort of activation we want to create. To do that, I took a sheet of paper and wrote down the things that mattered enough to me to want to make a difference to them. Perhaps these will be lofty goals, such as educating children, ending poverty, or more local tasks, like building a village community to be proud of. There's no right or wrong here; it's just about expressing it. If there is more than one thing, use a new sheet of paper for each.

Draw a line down the middle of the page, and on the left write everything you can think of that might make the difference you want to see. (I've learned that it is important not to judge their worth or the fit with current skills, but just to capture them.) On the right side, add one of these five words: 'Do', 'Teach', 'Learn', 'Fund', 'Ignore' – to highlight how you think you might be able to get involved.

I've found it more effective not to cross anything out, not to judge the results, and just to keep the paper handy. For a week or two I read them every day, adding to them with new thoughts.

What I found is that news stories, links on social media, conversations, all yielded new information and new thinking. I was adding to my notes for a while. But after a while the new material started to dry up. I decided that was a trigger to start honing the list, crossing out what I now realised I would ignore.

I decided what I would support by funding (supporting others to take action) should also be put to one side. From what was left, I started to take action, to make a difference immediately. Where sensible to do so, I would teach my skills to others so that I could multiply my impact and I sought out ideas and opportunities to learn what was needed to amplify that impact.

Ways to make a difference

1. In a similar way create your own documents, heading each sheet with something that is fundamentally important to you.

2. Imagine all the things that you could make a difference to that are on the left-hand side of the document, and decide if that is something you would do, teach, learn, fund or ignore.

3. Read the document every day, and add to it until you find it is no longer changing. Then decide what you will do as a result of the exercise, and, importantly, do it.

11 Taking Intentional Decisions and Actions

Dream big, start small, but most of all, start.

– Simon Sinek

First steps

Intent is a great word, derived originally from Latin, where the root means something being stretched, (hence also the modern English 'extended', which comes from the same root). Intent has come to mean something that has deliberate focus and commitment. On its own, though, that isn't enough.

There are many things which people intend to do but never get to. How often have you looked at your to-do list and wondered why you put some of the things on it that have stubbornly stayed there, undone? Of course, you had intent when you put them on the list; you had intent when you reviewed the list yesterday and the day before, when you still intended to do that thing. Yet you have not. Intent is not enough.

This chapter deals with intentional action. To move forward, we have to take steps, and if we take steps with intention then we will move forward with purpose. It's often as much the sense of progress that brings joy to our lives as the sense of completing something, concluding the journey. For some, the greatest joy is at the end; for others it is in the progress, and others still, in setting off. There is little joy in stagnation for anyone, and simply taking some action will always uncover insights that are needed for the journey.

Does that mean that any action is good enough? No. Without question, if you set off in the wrong direction then you will uncover insights that lock you into the wrong direction for too long. That's why taking intentional action is so important.

Bad debts

In the 2000s I had a client who brought me a significant proportion of my business's income, and I was able to attract others to work with me on their account. However, that contract came to an end when the clients sold the business, and a significant proportion of fees due to all their suppliers remained unpaid. My bad debt isn't the point of the story (although I learned a lot from the experience) but it is important for context. You can imagine that there was a lot of emotional reaction to the situation, especially when the consequences of it for the business were taken into account. Those who worked with me were paid what was due to them. Suffice to say that, for a period, as a result, my business struggled. Had I not had savings to rely on, the situation might have ended differently.

For too long I was enervated, unwilling to take any action, and doubting if I had the skills to do much anyway. As we discussed in Chapter 5, understanding and labelling those emotional reactions would have helped me to see what needed to be done, but I had yet to hone those skills. I was buffeted from one crisis to another, my work suffered, the service levels I was offering to others dropped and as a result clients found that I was no longer offering enough value for them to stay. Has something like that ever happened to you? It doesn't need to be such a traumatic event that triggers it, of course – these things can sneak up on us, as our imposter voice (see Chapter 2) challenges our right (or ability) to do business.

In the end, the business did turn around. I got the courage to start recognising my emotional depression and the impact it was having. I sought out ways to address the issue. I tried many things and a few of them started to work, and it was on those that I focused, with intent, and made them work harder. Gradually I started attracting clients again, their delight in the work that we did reinforcing the sensations of success and calming the imposter voice in my head. As the finances of the business started to be restored, so the ability that I had to build on the success and focus more intentionally on the right things was restored too. When I look back now, this time seems like a distant memory. While I wouldn't want you to have to go through something as traumatic, there was much learning for me. I hope, by sharing the story here, it will help you to avoid any setbacks you may have in your business.

What really made the difference was that, rather than being blown off course by external events, I started to take intentional action and focus on what I wanted to achieve.

Taking the right turn

The biggest of those learnings, for me, is that there is nothing that happens in any business without action, which is, naturally, a truism. A truism that has consequences though, and those consequences are not always obvious.

Actions move us – they take us from one state to another, one place to another. They always move us. We have to keep moving because our clients are also moving, and if we aren't moving too then, in the end, we cannot serve them. So a conscious choice to stand still will leave us in a place where the clients we already have will eventually choose to leave. The same is true of an unconscious choice. The same was true when my reaction to an external situation stagnated me.

It is always better to be intentional.

If we take action in *reaction* to external stimuli, sometimes turning right, sometimes turning left, there will be times when we move on the best path, and times when those actions take us away from it. There's a risk too, that, when we move on the wrong path, another situation will push us to take another action that moves us further away still. I think that is what happened to me over that difficult time. We have all heard comments such as 'They've lost their way', and that's nearly always because someone took just one wrong turn and then other things happened that shifted them again, further away. That's why your vision and goals are so important. Only with the clarity they bring can decisions be taken in the right framework and actions can be intentional.

Inaction, then, is a recipe for business disaster. The wrong action is the same, only perhaps even faster! We need, more often than not, to take actions that move us at least closer to the correct trajectory. (We need to do more than just that, but I'll come back to exactly what later.)

The question that poses for me, and perhaps for you too, is how can we do that with certainty, or at least with confidence, more often. In other words, how can we master that skill?

Application

Back when I was realising how far off track I had come, I started to explore my options. Not around what to do, but in how decisions are made and how to make better ones. I knew that too many of my decisions had been poor; I was asking the wrong questions and I was asking them badly. I decided that my route to a better business would always be easier if I asked better questions of myself and made better decisions.

Let's explore each of those elements.

Asking better questions, revisited

This is about the time I first came across the book I mentioned in Chapter 6.[32] *A More Beautiful Question* reminded me how important questions are as a starting point for thinking. A question that triggers thought can constrain it, or free it. Berger showed me that beautiful questions are rare, but asking them is a skill that can be honed and mastered. I worked hard at that, for in honing that skill I knew I would be solving a much bigger issue.

Reading the book was the start of that journey for me. I was an explorer again, but I quickly became a novice as my reading of the book built on my existing skills. I started to ask questions that acknowledged the situation but were not constrained by it. 'Given X. ...' had an impact on my imposter syndrome voice, in that it took away the 'but' that the doubter would throw into my thoughts. By having already acknowledged it, the 'but' has no residual power to cast doubt, and the question means it is exposed and being dealt with.

As my questioning skills reasserted themselves with the new knowledge from Berger's book, I found that I could spend time addressing the challenging (but often very simply expressed) questions I was posing. As I addressed them, new choices became apparent, choices I had thought I didn't have,

---

32 Berger, W. (2014). *A More Beautiful Question: The Power of Inquiry to Spark Breakthrough Ideas.* Bloomsbury.

choices that needed more thought if the decision was to be a good one.

Make better decisions

In every business, when we have our leadership hat on, we need to set the direction for the business. Having clarity of the intention, having a vision of the future state you seek, provides a framework for decision making. Then the decisions that are being considered can be tested against an objective standard of whether that decision moves the business toward or away from its stated objectives.

That is only a part of the story, of course – a decision can be aligned and still be poor.

It's also worth recognising that we have clarity about what the decision actually is. Often, a decision is made in isolation from its true place in the plans of the business. For example, if we decide to launch a new product, we are committing to time, effort and energy that has to be drawn away from other things we are doing.

In order to make better decisions it is important to check in with what we already know and verify that it is relevant to the situation. It's also important to validate the real truth of what we think we know. Sometimes that check-in highlights what we only thought we knew, and when we compare that to the actual facts we find our beliefs were misplaced. That happens much more often than most would estimate.

Decisions are also about giving something else up. Whenever we decide to do one thing, we are saying no to alternatives. It's important to really understand the consequences of that. For example, if we decide to invest in something for our business, we commit the financial resources for that investment. That money can only be spent once, so we cannot then do the other things that the money could have been used for.

We must also be aware of the cognitive biases that are always at work. Here are three we should always consider:

- **Confirmation bias**: this is the tendency to look for and find justification for the decision that we *want* to take. It's worth remembering that Google is not a source; it's an index that matches search terms to articles that contain that term. What it brings back is not verified; it's not necessarily factual – it's just there, available. We can address that in part by searching for the opposites and considering – validating – everything we find.

- **First-solution bias**: in a world where there are a million choices, the chances of you finding the best one first are pretty slim, however skilled you are. First-solution bias is the tendency to compare other choices to the first one. Partly because of primacy and the reality that the first solution has been in our minds the longest, it will feel most considered, most likely to succeed. We need to be more objective than that, and awareness of the bias is often all that is needed.

- **Authority bias:** Just because someone with more seniority or experience recommends a course of action does not mean it is right in your circumstances. Authority bias is the tendency not to check the details of their suggestion because we assume that they know already. Yet check we should, always.

It is also important to consider the timing: when does the decision have to be taken, and what information do we have by then? Chances are you won't have complete information, and delaying a decision in case more information comes to light can be just as damaging as taking it early and being aware of the information shortfalls. In many ways, all decision making is about being comfortable with some level of uncertainty. That means aiming to make 'good' decisions with imperfect knowledge.

Let's take a look at what defines a 'good' decision.

Quality

I do think it is important to be clear about how we measure the quality of a decision.

Let's take an example. I'm not a gambler, so I know very little about horse racing. If I was to go to a race meeting I might choose to back horse number 1 in each race. Over the course of the day I might win a couple of times and lose the rest. There is no difference in the quality of the decision to back horse 1 each time, but there is a difference in the outcome.

Yet often we judge the quality of our decisions on the outcome. That is a false assessment.

At the same race meeting you might find someone who is poring over form books, checking out the jockeys, looking at the horses in the parade ring, checking their weight and looking at the weather and ground conditions. Taking all that into account, they make their choice of which horse to bet on. The races run, they win and lose too, so are their decisions better? The likelihood is that they are, but it's not certain. They are certainly more informed, and if the information allows the decision to draw on experience from the past (e.g. on form) and to take account of the context of the present (e.g. track conditions) in ways which are known to improve the outcome, then the likelihood is that the decisions will be better.

In business too we can make better decisions by making them more informed with relevant contextual information.

What is a good decision? I prefer to define the quality of a decision by the inputs and the process, rather than the outcomes. That's not to say that you shouldn't measure the outcomes – of course you should! – and I'll discuss outcome measurement shortly.

We can measure the quality of our own decisions and we can follow a process to make better ones. I created a checklist for that process to ensure my bigger decisions are thought through. Here it is:

- What information do I have (that is relevant to the decision I need to take)?

- What information do I need to make this decision?

- Is there information that I need but do not yet have available? If so, when will it become available?

- What is my intended outcome, and how does this choice move me toward it?

- When must I take this decision, and when can I take it?

- What is the impact of not taking this decision?

- What will I give up with each option?

- How will I record the decision and my rationale?

- How, when and why will I measure the outcomes?

When I work with clients I record the decisions that they reach from our work and validate how they are panning out over time. That's a key part of how people move from being practical decision-makers to expert or master decision-makers.

The quality of a decision is really a measure of whether you took the decision with as much information as you could acquire and an appropriate consideration of the consequences. That definition doesn't refer to outcomes at all.

Measuring outcomes

Of course, we also need to measure results so we know the outcomes of the decisions we are taking. Measurement could be the subject of a chapter on its own, which isn't relevant to our purpose here. Suffice to say I'll stick to some guidelines that work well for me.

First, don't measure things because they are easy to measure; measure what matters. For example, measuring how many people visit your website is easy (just put an analytics service on it), but is it meaningful? In some contexts it might be, but in most it's really not relevant. (Measuring something that *might* be useful, just in case, is a fool's errand – you'll waste time recording and thinking about the data, but the chance that you will need it is limited.)

Second, don't measure things that won't change your decision or trigger any action.

Third, measure things that will change your decision and trigger action based on the outcome. Define the actions and rationale for all the possible outcomes of that measure in advance, as that will simplify your response to the outcomes as they develop.

With these outcome-focused measurements, you can truly test how effective a decision was, but, as we have discussed, not the quality of the decision making.

Experience decisions

Masters know something about decisions that experts often miss. They have insights that come from their wisdom. They know, from all their experience, skill and knowledge, the success or otherwise of decisions in the past. They seem instinctively to know when the right moment to commit is, and they are prepared to take *managed* risk, which mitigates the uncertainty that remains.

The real point is that they are intentional about every decision. They know how it moves them or their business forward and how well aligned they are to the long-term objectives of both. They understand who needs to be involved and they involve them at just the right time.

How do they do that?

They have a great cache of data and experience and their mastery gives them insights that can improve decision making. Yet, if we are not yet masters, what can we learn from that to help us make the journey? Their experience came from somewhere – it didn't come out of books, or from listening to others – it came from making decisions and honing the skill of doing so. It came because they were intentional *all the time*. They act with clear intent and a desire to achieve it, and they take decisions aligned to that intent and with the best information possible.

Even with limited skills we can start to do that and gather the experience as a result. We will learn from that experience and grow our understanding of, and improve, our decision-making capabilities.

If we are to be building better business we need to be taking better decisions too. We also need to follow up those decisions with intentional action. Even when we do that, we still may not always get the result we want every time, but we will get a better result more often. Some will not work, but others will exceed our expectations.

Ways to master decision making

1. Make your decisions intentionally, and ensure that you know how they align with your vision for the business. Use the checklist from earlier in the chapter as a guide.

2. Keep a log and record in it information about the important decisions that are intended to change the shape of your business. By recording the decision, the alternatives that were considered, the risks and opportunities involved and the costs, you will gradually build up a body of knowledge that will help you to understand your own decision making style, and improve it.

3. Analyse the outcomes of your decisions (and for the important decisions record them in your decision log). Find out why things worked or why they did not. Only then can our decisions and the actions that flow from them help us to build our mastery, from what we learn.

12 Sharing Insights and Skills

*A small group of thoughtful people
could change the world.*

– Margaret Mead

Depth and breadth

As you develop your expertise and put in place the strategies here, you will find that your results become more consistent and reliable. You will also learn much about why things work as they do and see how to take them from one context and apply them in another. That cross-contextual understanding is a key part of building expertise and mastery. It's a truism that in order to know more and more about a topic and get depth, we have to narrow the breadth. Focusing on a narrower skill facilitates getting better at it until we become an expert, then *the* expert and then master.

David Smith revisited

In the introduction to this book I talked about David Adrian Smith and how he had decided to sell his sign-writing business (less specific) to focus on glass etching, gilding and letter writing (more specific). Like any master of his skill, he now also trains, coaches, teaches, cajoles and motivates others to follow in his footsteps. David Adrian Smith didn't simply emulate the skills of those who taught him. He took their skills, learned them, honed them, and put them together in new ways and in his style. That's what he wants his students to do too, and it's what I want you to do as a result of reading this book.

Perspective

Business is always evolving. We learn all the time and in our own ways put together the knowledge that we have, the skills that we have honed and the experience we have had into the mix in order to see where it takes us. Our minds are extraordinary; they see patterns and use them to give meaning to what is around us. Each of us ends up with our own patterns, each of us with our own history, each of us seeing things from a slightly different perspective.

That reality means we each have a unique set of insights that give us a view on the world that others simply cannot have. I've often argued that there is no unique selling proposition for any product that has ever been sold, but if there was something unique it would last a few moments after exposure to the public gaze. What is unique is each of us. Our individual take on the world, our own knowledge, skill, experience and, for the masters, insights, that no one else can have.

Creating a community

That uniqueness brings with it a responsibility, doesn't it? We can let it simply be used in the service of clients, adding value where it can, or we can do that *and* make sure that it lasts beyond our time. Not unaltered of course, as we will discuss, but always part of the history of the markets we are in. To make it last we have to share what we know with others, and we need to keep learning from others too. I've found it useful to think in terms of having a community of like-minded people who share some element of the vision you have and support you as you achieve the mastery of your work.

Mastery groups

The limits of your capability

In 1937 Napoleon Hill wrote *Think and Grow Rich*.[33] In that book (in Chapter 10) he says, 'Economic advantages may be created by any person who surrounds himself with the advice, counsel, and personal cooperation of a group who are willing to lend him wholehearted aid, in a spirit of perfect harmony.' He goes on to talk about the psychic energy that is generated when several minds come together to consider the issues and opportunities that face them. Hill acknowledges that much of his thinking was shaped by Dale Carnegie, and to some extent by Henry Ford. What is clear though is that a group is always much more powerful than the individuals within it.

I'll come on to describe how the Mastermind groups that I've been involved with have worked, and how their collective wisdom has been a part of what has given me the insights to be able to write this book. Suffice to say at this point how much of what I have been able to develop came about because of sharing thoughts with others and listening to their ideas and thoughts in return. One person's experience often triggers thoughts by others that, when verbalised in the right way, allow a third to identify connections and contexts that would otherwise remain opaque. It is extraordinary.

---

33 Hill, N. (2008). *Think and Grow Rich*. Tarcherperigee.

Would Hill understand and recognise the groups that exist to do this today? I think he would, for there are fundamental principles at work that do not change much, or at all, over time. That's because they are about the interaction of people, and how their thinking works together. Neuroscience is beginning to comprehend the mechanisms that do this, and those mechanisms are part of what it means to be alive, part of the human condition.

I've alluded in the title to mastery groups, and I should probably provide some background to that. For me, as you'll see in the next few pages, mastery groups are not just a gathering of a few people. They are not a 'talking shop'. They have purpose and intention behind them: a collective community spirit that makes them something very special for their members. In many groups, taking in new members is difficult (or even impossible) because of the depth of relationships that already exist. Deep and enduring friendships are one of the key consequences of their existence. That does not happen by accident, it happens by design.

Mastery groups are not for the fainthearted; members will be challenged to stretch and reach beyond the current limits of their capability. They will focus on business results, on creating and building better business for their members, and encouraging and facilitating their individual mastery. They achieve this by discussing, in a structured process, the opportunities they have. They encourage deeper thinking, better decisions, and have the advantage of also providing a level of accountability that encourages and motivates. In general this focuses on decisions of what to do and the ability to draw on collective experience to know how to do it.

Mastery groups take collective working a stage further. They look at each member, at their knowledge, skills, experience and insights, and support them as they make the transition to being a master of what they do. Mastery groups lift those who are already expert in what they do to the higher level of mastery. When you can do that, you will be sought out by those seeking your talent, and the premium you can charge for your refined expertise will rise. Commercially, mastery groups both accelerate and magnify success.

BlackStar

A few years ago I led a community of small business owners known as BlackStar, part of an online community called Ecademy. Working with the CEO, Glenn Watkins, we implemented groups, a forerunner of mastery groups, as part of the offering to members of BlackStar. In order to deliver the best value we developed a process to use when those groups met. Over the years that followed I've revised that concept to take into account the learning that has been possible from facilitating such groups, and from being a member of others.

My group

In 2017 I asked a small group of close friends who also ran active businesses if they would like to work together in a business group, and it has been a rock for me ever since. We meet about every six weeks, and I have seen us all support each other in a whole host of ways that go far beyond business connections. Separation, miscarriage, opportunities to take big jobs, navigating the pandemic, frustrations with suppliers and more have all appeared in our discussions in the last few years. Yet in all that we have all been able to be more resilient, more focused, more able to cope than we would have been had we not all been working and getting to know each other so well.

It's unusual for any of us to bring something to the group that we have seen before, but it's also unusual for all of the group to be unaware of a situation that doesn't have parallels and similarities with their own. As a result we are able to bring our experience to bear in ways that may not even be conceivable to the person initiating the discussion. Almost every time we discuss an opportunity or challenge there will be elements of it that the person who brings it up simply will not have thought of at all. A different facet perhaps, a different lens that gives someone the opportunity to think in different and new ways.

Another aspect of the group is that, every time we have a discussion, there is opportunity for everyone to learn. We all build our understanding from the knowledge, skills, experience and insights of the others in the group. At the moment we learn something from each other it may not be immediately relevant, but it forms a part of our deeper understanding of our own businesses and adds value to each of us as a result. I've been surprised how often something I thought of as little more than 'interesting' when we had the discussion in the group then became game-changing when something happened later.

My group has brought home to me how important a part of mastery it is to be surrounded by the people to whom you can turn when it is needed, and to be willing to reach out to them.

The practical alternative to work

When it comes to business discussions, I've often joked that meetings are the 'practical alternative to work'. Mastery meetings are never that, and they never feel like it, either. They do, though, require some commitments from all those who participate in them. Without those commitments, the chance of the group being sustainable and valuable for everyone is reduced.

For me and for the clients that I work with in mastery groups, I think these are the most important of those commitments:

- **Turn up.** That sounds simple, and yet for so many groups there is a lack of willingness from some to actually turn up for the meetings. Of course, there are always some things that will take precedence, and people have to miss a meeting now and again. But not putting it in your diary, not scheduling around it, is an indication that the person just isn't right for the group.

- **It's not (just) about you.** The group is the important thing, so focus on others first and they will look after you.

- **Learning matters, not teaching.** Sometimes in groups there's someone who is there because they think they know the answer. While all of us may know *an* answer, it's unlikely that we know *the* answer for sure, and in discussion new insights will improve it anyway. So, come with a mindset of wanting to learn rather than to teach.

- **Respect the process.** Every group will develop a process that works for them. Whatever that process is, it's there because it is the best the group has at the moment. For sure make suggestions to improve it, but until you all agree, respect what you have.

- **Pass it on.** How can you take what you know and pass it on to others so that they can take it, and in their turn, develop it?

Facilitated process

A mastery group works because of the people in the group, but that alone is not enough. They need a process, and that process needs to be facilitated. Without both of those elements they will always descend into talking shops. They will stop being a mastery group, and after some time, will fall apart. Let's look at both of those elements.

The process

In a mastery group there is a series of 'rounds' with one person in the 'hot seat' where they bring a topic that they want to discuss with the group. The group will generally follow a process that goes something like this:

1. **Context:** A short period for the person to describe the topic and provide some contextual background. When people are experienced in these sessions, they recognise that the next section will elicit what others want and need to know, so this is more about simply providing a reference point.

2. **Exploration:** The second element is an exploration. Questions flow from the others in the group to the topic holder to explore it more deeply. These questions should be open (seeking a narrative answer rather than a yes or no answer) and should not be solution-focused. The facilitator is important here, and their skill in reframing some of the questions into a more useful format is important, especially when people are new to the group or the topic.

3. **Restatement:** During the questions, the topic holder often finds that their understanding of the topic has changed, and it is important for them to be able to reframe the

question they are asking of the group. This allows the next section to be much more relevant to the topic holder.

4. **Solutions:** This section is an opportunity for the participants to feed back and make suggestions for the topic holder. It's important that, during this section, the topic holder does not respond, interrupt or distract from the opinions being shared. Sometimes they will hear some hard truths, sometimes things which they think have already been shown not to be relevant and the temptation to speak can be strong. It should be resisted. The insights and value of the feedback can often be in the subtlety and nuance of the thoughts offered, and that needs time for the whole solution to be given, and for it to be considered. Once the solutions have been offered, the topic holder may ask for clarification or expansion on any aspect of what they have heard.

5. **Actions:** In this section the topic holder commits to whatever actions they feel they will take forward. These are recorded, and the group will expect an update on how things developed either at the next meeting or during an interim communication.

6. **Mastery:** Nearly all topics are brought to the group because the member doesn't currently have mastery of that aspect yet, so this section will identify and highlight four key areas for them to explore. What knowledge do they (or did they before the session) need? What skills do they need to hone? What experience do they need to have? Finally, by the time of the next session, the topic holder is expected to update the group on the insights that arose as a result of the development of additional knowledge, skills and experience in the first three areas. It is these insights that lift the whole group toward a greater understanding and wisdom. Toward mastery.

As a group, we are looking beyond the solution to allow the business to advance as a result of the solution as applied. We are also looking for how that advance can become a permanent, resilient, reliable part of the business. This is because the focus is less on what to do and how to do it, and more about facilitating that it is done.

The facilitator

An important element of any mastery group is its facilitation. This has to be light touch, and yet highly skilled. Light touch, because the important aspects are the topic and the outcome, rather than rigidity to the process. Highly skilled so that there is intention in knowing when it is wise to go 'off piste' and allow some latitude from the process, and when to get back on track.

During the exploration phase, the facilitator's role can make or break the value of the sessions. Time is always short, as almost every question, if well formed, will open up thinking for both the questioner and the group. It is easy for the discussion to head down alleyways, rabbit holes and irrelevances, but sometimes such diversions lead to new and deeply valuable understanding. As a result, it is important for the facilitator to use their judgement on how far to let the discussion stray from the originally stated topic. They will also recognise when the stated topic may be changing. The skill of the facilitator is to identify when the topic holder is feeling content with where the business is going, and when they are not. The facilitator must use their experience in knowing when to stick with a line of questioning that is uncomfortable, and when to divert to safe ground for a period to let the emotional impacts from the session settle. Part of that skill is exhibited in the way that they can reframe questions to maintain the intention of the person asking while also ensuring that the question is open, not solution focused and non-judgemental. Question design is not a skill that many have mastered, but in the facilitator, it is essential for the effective operation of a mastery group.

Taking the final step

Mastery groups are designed to help with the final steps of the journey to mastery by allowing members of the group to collectively uncover the insights that move an individual from deep expertise to mastery. That is often a deeply emotional shift. As practitioners, we are often proud of what we do, and rightly so, because we do it well. As experts, we are proud of how we do it because the experiences have been hard won. Masters are proud of the difference they make to others. This shift, when it happens, is deeply affecting; it can be accompanied by tears and a sense of deep understanding.

There is also a realisation, along with the pride, that there is more of the journey to go. More insights to gather and more depth to understand, for that is the reality of the pursuit of mastery: there is more to do. The deeply emotional impact of seeing this for the first time is as powerful as falling in love. It is the moment when people truly connect with a sense of purpose, and an understanding of their 'why'.

Pass it on

David Adrian Smith is as keen today to pass on his skills, perhaps keener, as he is to use them for clients. He knows, as we all do, that our time on this planet is limited, but he also knows that his skills are transferable, his knowledge is teachable, his experience is shareable and his insights are valuable.

A key part of mastery is having sufficient knowledge, honed skills, long-standing experience, and the insights to pass it on to others. As masters we can take pride in sharing with others and from the difference that we will make to them.

Flashes of mastery

I think that everyone running a business with some success will have insights and flashes of mastery around some aspect of what they do, and what the business does. Our challenge is to make that mastery become embedded every day. When you do that, you will make the business very special, to make it the only business to do what it does *your way*.

In my experience the single biggest thing any of us can do, as masters of our own art, is to teach what we know to others. The process of teaching requires a level of thinking that goes beyond understanding and into the world of how to transfer understanding to another person. We only have the limited tools of the language and our ability to demonstrate. When we work on making that effective it has always, in my experience, deepened knowledge of the subject, unlocked and uncovered additional insights and clarified the rationale.

Those things alone make it worth spending time working out how to teach something even if you don't (yet) have any students. There is another aspect to this too: teaching is collaborative, not distributive. By that, I mean that it's not just about the teacher passing on their knowledge (that's pedagogic learning – what we do in school – it lifts people from explorer to novice). When masters teach experts it becomes deeply collaborative. The insights flow both ways; the expert is lifted by the master who, like a boat on a rising tide, is lifted by the experience and insights they both get. Teaching someone who is already an expert is about far more than sharing knowledge – the teaching is about the sharing of insight, drawn from the experience of using deeply honed skills.

Ways to share with others

1. Write about what you do so that others can understand your knowledge and skill.

2. Speak about your topic. The work involved in preparing talks will make sure you think about how others learn best from you.

3. Join a peer or a mastery group.

13 Being Yourself

To be yourself in a world that is constantly trying to make you something else is the greatest accomplishment.

– Ralph Waldo Emerson

Labels

Over many years I've been many things: a son, a brother, a husband, a student, an underwriter, a risk manager, a business owner, a mentor, a photographer, a walker. All labels, all trying to put a box around me for the circumstances in which the label is useful. None of them are wrong, but neither are they complete.

Identity

I mentioned earlier the impact that the Masterclass video course by Jimmy Chin, the adventure photographer, had on me. On the same site is another course by Annie Leibovitz, the portrait photographer. In both those classes, neither master spent much time – if any – on the mechanics of taking photographs, nor on the equipment. Neither focused on one's skills in taking photographs nor how to use the equipment more effectively; they focused on the mastery they had, the insights and the ways of thinking that are needed to *be* a photographer. Their courses were as much about identity as they were about skill.

While Jimmy Chin is famous for images that have been used in magazines like *National Geographic*, much of his work is also commissioned by brands to support advertising and marketing. He showed us in easy-to-understand terms how these two requirements differ and how they require different kinds of thinking. Thinking about what you are trying to achieve and having a plan before even picking up the camera is, I think, one of the key differences between those who enjoy their photography as a hobby and those who enjoy it for what it lets them be.

Annie Leibovitz is famous for black and white portraiture, always using light in unusual or different ways to create a highlight here, a shadow there. Her composition tells unusual and important stories about the subject. Her photography is intimate, personal, unique to her. It's very special.

More recently, British photographer Rankin was the lead judge in a BBC competition to find the best British photographer. Again, what was really being taught was not how to take better photographs, but how to be, how to think, how to behave and how to build relationships as – and care about being – a photographer.

In the introduction I referenced David Adrian Smith and his journey of apprenticeship with master letter-writer Gordon Farr and then later with master guilder Rick Glawson. All of these masters – David Smith, Rick Glawson, Gordon Farr, Jimmy Chin, Rankin and Annie Leibovitz – have something in common; their pleasure in their skill, which they all still strive to improve, to develop further and to understand in more detail. Yet this is only a part of who they are. Another is knowing that there is much to pass on, which they do willingly. For some masters, it becomes the main thing they do.

It's worth reflecting on David Adrian Smith's journey for a moment. He didn't become a clone of Gordon Farr - nor, I suspect, would Gordon have wanted him to. David learned from him and mastered in his own style what was useful to his own journey to mastery. Later, he layered on the skills of gilding and glass etching. David now passes his skills on to others in courses and one-to-one work with those who wish to learn from him. Those students will not be clones either; they will take his skill, learn it, and then make it their own, layering it with the experience they get, and the other masters they engage with as part of their journeys. This is a complex dance, but the steps are easy to understand, and hard to master.

Extraordinary talent

You are the combination of what you know, what you are skilled at and what you have experienced. You are also a product of how you think about each of those. You uncover insights that come from thinking about the way aspects of what you know and are skilled at affect you and others. Thinking about what those skills enable you to achieve, for yourself and others, and the experiences you have as you achieve them, enables you to build deeper understanding.

It's a truism that depth is not superficial, but you cannot be a master without depth, and we cannot achieve depth if we hang on to too much of the superficial. Here is another important point: in the world we find ourselves in, most people are generalists - they know about a lot of things and apply many skills in their day-to-day activity and work.

To become masters we need to find the depths, understand the detail and be able to use it in many contexts - finding ways to share the insights we gain along the way. We will know more and more about what we do until it becomes a part of who we are.

If you take photographs for money, as you learn the art you will become a photographer, but as you master it you will become a landscape photographer, or an adventure photographer, or a wedding photographer – or some other specialism. As you reach the pinnacle of your skill you might become an adventure photographer known for extraordinary shots from some of the world's toughest environments. That's a soubriquet that might well be applied to Jimmy Chin. He is not just a master photographer, but also a climber of extraordinary talent, a skier willing to take on the hardest descents, and a film director. It is the combination of his mastery of each of these skills that makes him who he is. Who are you?

Gravitas

As Ralph Waldo Emerson said (and I've included it as the opening quotation for this chapter), being yourself is not easy. The world will want you to be many things, and for many of them you are not best placed to take on that mantle. To be true to who you are requires a focus and dedication; yet for those that achieve it, there is something else. Described variously as confidence, gravitas or presence, it is a characteristic we all recognise when we see it. It is the signature of a master.

Let's look at why that happens. As we move through the journey to mastery we tend to encounter others at the top of their game. We have learned how to do what we do, but we haven't necessarily honed our expertise or had the time and resources to really consider all aspects of it, garnering the insights that come from such deep reflection. As we work with, or are mentored by, those whose skills complement and align with our own, we start to pick from their understanding what matters in our own world. When David Adrian Smith worked as an apprentice with Gordon Farr, he learned all about hand-drawn letter writing and honed the same skills. He did not learn everything that Gordon Farr knew – that would take a lifetime – nor did he emulate his style. He took those parts of what he knew were necessary for him to make his own journey. Under Farr's guidance he could create his own style, and he did.

Who is it that you are learning from? Perhaps you're working formally, because they're engaged as a mentor, coach, consultant, guide or partner, or informally because you are observing them from afar. In my own journey I've learned to ask a few questions that help me home in on what I want to develop as my own skill set. Thinking of the people who I see as masters in their field and from whom I wish to learn, I ask:

- What is it about what they do or say, or the way they work, that I admire?

- Why is that important for my own development?

- What do they not do that I might need to stop doing, and what impact will that have?

- What do they do that I know nothing or little about, and how can I learn more?

- Who will I become when I have succeeded in learning all I can from them?

What you will become

In the early stages of writing this book I was asked by my coach, the wonderful Caroline Southerden, one of the questions that only a great coach can ask. A question that opens up thinking and draws out something quite special. She asked me: 'In the context of writing a book, what would you ask one of your clients to best understand their aims from that work?' I pondered for a while and started with, 'Why are you writing it?' But we both knew that was weak, and laughed.

'What do you want your readers to think?' Better, but still not good enough.

'What do you want your readers to do?' No, still not there. Back and forth we went, trying out questions that didn't hit at the essence of what someone who was a master, writing a book to support others on the journey they had taken, would want.

Then it came:

'What do you want your readers, as a result of reading your book, to become?'

Mastery is about identity, about who you are as a person, about how you show up every day, and every minute of every day. I want you, when you have read this book, to be in a position to decide what you will master, and why it's important to you. I want that so that you can be the best you that you can be. I want you to be building better business by mastering the elements you choose (and surrounding yourself with masters of the elements that your business needs but that you do not wish to, or cannot, master). I want you to be fully yourself. Only you can judge if this book achieves that aim.

Who will you become tomorrow?

Appletree

It's important to recognise where you want to go, having real clarity about what you want to hone and develop as a master.

Working with Chantal Cornelius, a marketing expert who focuses on supporting coaches, consultants and trainers, we discussed how her business, Appletree, has developed since it was founded more than 21 years ago. Initially she focused on supporting her clients with practical marketing design and the provision of marketing services, such as producing written content for newsletters. The business was providing practitioner services to those whose marketing knowledge was slim. Over time, as her expertise developed, she began mentoring others to be proficient at marketing their own businesses, and her client base changed as a result. It also meant her fees rose as her reputation as an expert grew. We discussed where she needed to develop and grow her expertise to develop the mastery we both knew was beginning to blossom.

Chantal loves marketing: it's part of who she is, and always has been, but her joy is compounded and magnified as she deepens her knowledge, hones her skills and gathers experience.

In our discussions we identified one aspect of her work, an important one, that will allow her to be seen for her mastery in the next phase of her business. She understands the importance of the way the emotions customers feel defines the business's reputation in the market. When her clients understand that and reflect it in their marketing, it will sing for them. Chantal's research is uncovering more important connections every day as her mastery develops.

Here is the depth I was speaking of earlier. For her, and for you, once you identify the areas where your insights have unlocked something powerful, you must dig deeper, understand it in all its aspects and guises and test out your insights in the real world to see how they work.

A side note: you also must be wary of confirmation bias in that work; you have to be willing to be wrong, very wrong, because sometimes you will be. So try to break your theory as well as trying to understand it. No, really – try hard to break it and don't be disappointed if you do, because in the break is opportunity and learning. Even if you do break your initial understanding of your insights, it's very rare that you will not find new understanding and new insights to test as a result. Indeed, it is the experience of knowing when your insights break that will, ultimately, give you the edge over those who will copy you and claim your expertise. There's a reason the original is usually best, so stick at it.

Understanding your mastery is about understanding all aspects of that part of what you do that is at the heart of who you are.

Ways to master action

1. Identify those parts of what you do that you can explore in more detail and research them carefully.

2. Consider your current ways of working. Are you working with explorers and novices so they become practitioners or are you working with practitioners and experts to lift their game further? How would you like your business to change as you develop mastery?

3. Set aside time to research and develop your own skills. Do not be afraid of investing significantly in your own development; the returns will come.

4. Who are you today, who will you become tomorrow?

---

14 What's Next?

I always tell my kids if you lay down,
people will step over you. But if you keep scrambling,
if you keep going, someone will always,
always give you a hand. Always. But you gotta keep
dancing, you gotta keep your feet moving.

– Morgan Freeman

Looking back

One day, you will look back and remember where you have come from and at all you have achieved. You will look in wonder at the mastery that you have reached. I mentioned Steve Jobs' commencement speech earlier in this book, and in that he talks about only being able to join the dots while looking back. You can see the journey you have taken and how the pieces fit together when you look back over a lifetime of achievements – your achievements. For some, there will be a moment of relief that the work is done, and they will relax. Not you. This journey does not end; it takes us onward, and it will always take us onward. For those who choose mastery, it is exciting to know that the very best is always yet to come.

Pista per sciatori esperti

We were in Cortina, skiing on a gentle blue ski run toward the junction, shown on the piste map as the start of a route called simply 'black 51' but known locally as the 'James Bond run' – a long and steep run made famous by the James Bond film *For Your Eyes Only*. We turned toward it to be greeted by a sign with the words 'Pista per sciatori esperti' – piste for expert skiers. I was skiing with a long-time ski partner with similar skills to mine. We had seen the run from afar as we had been coming up the mountain. Its narrow entrance and steep start were picturesque and the nature of the run meant it was not heavily used. It was likely we would be heading down alone. Neither of us regularly skied runs this difficult, but we had both managed to get down some hard slopes in recent years and felt our skiing had improved. We were ready, physically at least. Mentally, both of us were nervous – we were going into a little bit of the unknown, in a country we had not skied in before and at a resort we didn't know – heading to a world-famous black run that many who could manage it would still choose to avoid.

I paused to take a picture of the sign. In reality, I was pausing because I wanted to overcome my fears by giving them time to subside. My ski buddy, though, overcomes her fears by not giving them time to grow – by getting on with it. In this moment our coping techniques worked against each other. Fight or flight, it was time to go. So we did.

The very top of the slope is extraordinarily steep: the ground falls away in a parabola, so you are lulled for a moment into thinking it will be just a little steeper than what you are used to. It's not. It keeps on getting steeper – 52 degrees at its steepest – just for a few yards. Turn, pick the next spot, shift the weight, keep focus on the slope, letting the hips and skis work in harmony, and the edges keep you in control – just. Turn, turn again, turn again, turn, turn, turn and relax. A level area. Ski to a stop, turn one last time and look back – and up. Wow. That. We just skied that. The laughter comes easily.

Are we master skiers? No, for sure we are not. We have much to learn, and yet we have a love of it and a level of mastery. Expert enough to not just manage to get down this run, but to enjoy it too, to be confident, to be in the moment and to know how to ski it, and to take time to still be honing our skills and thinking about the next time.

Over the edge

In business too I have often found myself at the equivalent of the top of the James Bond run in Cortina, knowing I am pushing boundaries, going further, possibly going farther, risking being a little bit on the edge, or perhaps a bit beyond the line of control. Knowing that I will look back at what has been done and think, 'Wow – that! We just did that!' There's something else here though, something quite subtle and hidden until you spot it. I've never had that feeling alone.

Sometimes I've been with a master and they have lifted my performance, so I stretch; sometimes I've been with the less skilled and lifted them. In those cases my joy is at their success, their achievement, their delight. So often in my mentoring work what is achieved is done by my client, enabled by the encouragement I've given, facilitated by the strategies we jointly developed, but achieved by their taking the step off the edge, making the turns, doing the work.

A long time ago a mentor of mine, Des Robertson, highlighted how in sport the team manager, the coach, was not the person who lifted the trophy, and yet we all know that without their mastery, the success would not be there. Masters enable others to achieve beyond their previous capabilities, lifting and supporting them to set off and highlighting the successes as they come.

When the mastery is there, do masters stop? Never. The learning goes on, and there is mastery within mastery, within mastery. The black belt is not the end of the journey; it is also layered with more of the same journey. Someone achieving a level of mastery today is little more than an explorer of their mastery. Soon they will be a novice master, and so on, until they step up another level and start exploring new insights afresh.

This is, to all intents and purpose, what we are all on this earth to strive for. It is our raison d'être, our why. To be the best that we can be at what we specialise in doing, and then to be better still. To strive, to achieve, to lift our game, lift it further and lift it again. Tomorrow you will do more, and be more, than you are today.

Don't keep the home fires burning

I'm not suggesting that this is some arduous, never-ending drudgery that simply must be plodded through day by day, week by week, year by year. Not some toil we look back on and wonder why we bothered to start. Too often this is the lot of people who have not yet seen the value of honing their skills and focusing on just those areas where they can be exceptional. Yes, your journey is an ongoing one, yet you know it will never be the same. It is always better, always more valuable, more insightful, more joyful.

Too often I've seen business leaders taking on work they are capable of, but which is not directly in their area of expertise, and struggling. They can do the work, make a return and, therefore, keep the home fires burning – but the work does not light their own fire. They do it because times are hard, or because they don't want to miss an opportunity. Too often each of these opportunities leads them further away from their core purpose, partly because it is educating the market about what is being done, not the thing that they wish to do.

If this book stops you doing that, then I will have achieved my aim. It is so important that I can't begin to stress it enough. Your joy of mastery can only come if you choose to master what it is that you do, in the very precise area of what that is. Do choose that, and be dedicated to it. If you do, you will become the master that you deserve to be. Probably not this week, perhaps not this year – but you will get there.

Focus

A focus on mastery means taking risks, putting your abilities on the line and seeing if they can take you to your goal. A focus on mastery means turning away from things that don't align with the journey you are taking. That focus will achieve much, and like David Adrian Smith you will be found by those people who know they need *just* what you do, in *just* the way you do it because they want to benefit from what you have mastered. When they do, that is when you'll be rewarded for all the choices you made.

You have probably got the impression the journey to mastery that I want you to take can be difficult, at times; that it can need dedication and effort, and that is true. But I also want to be clear that for most of the time it is also a joy because it is aligned to you. Aligned to who you are and who you will be. Continuing the journey makes you who you will become. Those moments, when you look back at what you have achieved, just as I did as we came down the James Bond run, and see what has happened, will fill your heart with pride and make your soul soar.

When that happens, and it will, I'd invite you – as I do regularly – to ask 'What's next?' and to think about how you can use what you have become to reach out to others, to make a difference, and to pass it on.

Ways of intentional mastery

1. Decide, in exquisite detail, what is the next thing you will truly master.

2. Honestly deconstruct your current situation and ask what single element you lack that would immediately improve it.

3. Seek out the best way to make that improvement and commit wholeheartedly to it.

4. Review, reflect and redefine.

You will have fun while you do those things, and I hope that every day is filled with joy.

Making a Dent

It always seems impossible until it's done.

– Nelson Mandela

During my two main careers, both in the insurance industry and as a mentor, I've been deeply impressed by the masters who supported and influenced me. While all of them did what they do at least in part to make a living, they all sought to be building better business. That was merely the point of entry into something more far reaching for them.

When I worked at Lloyds TSB in the late 1990s, I was impressed by the efforts put in by members of staff in their own time, in the support of others. Lloyds TSB operated a foundation which received a proportion of the bank's profits. Prior to 2008, those profits were significant and the contribution to the foundation was similarly generous. Staff were encouraged to contribute to causes which were important to them. The foundation would match any financial commitment the staff member was able to make themselves or to raise through their efforts, and those contributions were doubled.

When I left Lloyds TSB and started my own business, I knew that, with the best will in the world, my financial contribution would always be much more limited than was possible with the power of the Lloyds TSB foundation.

Yet when I look at the business landscape I can see just how many small businesses there are. What if there was a pooling of resources? What if each contributed a small part of their revenues? What if they could each spare just one person for a week or so each year to work on projects? If only a small proportion of the small business community were moved to take part, these resources would constitute a massive movement. What sort of difference could we all make together?

In the body of the book, I discussed the foundation that one of my clients, Speak First – a training business, set up to build floating classrooms in Bangladesh to ensure that children could be taught even in the monsoon. One small business, through their commitment, achieved something meaningful. How much more could be done if 10 or 20 similar sized businesses chipped in to build more classrooms?

Mastery has many consequences. It teaches you not just what you can do, but how you can then influence and motivate others to achieve because of your insight. Mastery means you will have the ability to see things you understand in one context and rationalise how they will play out in another. Mastery has a habit of encouraging us to go deeper, to shed the less relevant parts of what we know in order to focus on what is more relevant to us. Yet when we have that depth of knowledge in that narrow area that we understand so well, we can and will pass it on to others who are creating their own framework, to use it in their own way and hone it for their own expertise and mastery in their turn. This is how the human race moves forward.

As a final thought I'd ask you to consider a few questions, things that may trigger some further ideas and thoughts for you:

1. What is it that I really want to be the best at?

2. Who else is at the top of that game? What can I learn from them?

3. What can I see from my mountaintop that others cannot?

4. What insights do I get from that view?

5. Where do I want to go next?

Practitioners are in the engine room; they keep the status quo as the status quo, they make organisations work, practically, day to day, every day. Experts improve things within the context of what they are. As a master you will be leading change, using the knowledge you have learned, and you'll create the opportunities to make a difference way beyond your business. Perhaps to children in a far-off country or to your local community. Whatever matters to you is what matters to us all.

I wrote this book because I know that when the knowledge within is applied by you in your world and in your way, we can together make a difference that really does make a difference.

With your mastery, it is our future.

Acknowledgements

First, I'd like to thank you for reading this book. I hope that it has inspired you to take action so that your future mastery drives you to be building better business every day.

When I decided to write this book, my first thought was to devise it as a letter to my daughter, Frances, to help her with her career that was just starting when I first put pen to paper. Published on her birthday, I hope she draws strength and insight from this book for many years.

This learning would not have been possible without the work I have done with clients and all the people I have worked with and admired throughout my career. From Bill, my first mentor, to those I work with now in my own mastery group, Lee Warren, Heidi Ashley, Kelly Molson and Simon George, who are all an inspiration to me.

The publishing team at the Right Book Company – Sue, Paul, Andrew, Jane and others – have been brilliantly professional and a marvellous support for me. This book is so much better than it would have been without your masterful work. As part of that, I am so grateful for the creation of the Right Book Buddies and our team of Kate, Nadine, Ceri, Richard, Mike, Nick, David, Darren and Jan who often worked together on collaborative Zoom calls through the trials of the pandemic. Your spirits, your joy, your skills and your experience – all showed me what can be achieved collectively. I know that the writing we have all done has, and will continue to, change lives across the globe. Thank you for your company and insights.

Many others have played a part in making this book better as it developed. Chantal Cornelius's insights have been pivotal; my coach Caz Southerden, whose skilled, insightful questioning was extraordinary; Ben Fedrick, a master physiotherapist, kept me physically fit; Caroline Cavanagh kept me sane. My good friends Nicky, Charlotte and Siobhan gave me the honour of time to think.

Finally, David Adrian Smith, your work is extraordinary, and I am honoured to have begun to get to know you. Thank you.